NEWCASTLE/BLOODAXE POETRY SERIES: 16

ANNE STEVENSON

About Poems

and how poems are not about

NEWCASTLE / BLOODAXE POETRY LECTURES

BLOODAXE BOOKS

ISBN: 978 1 78037 345 4

First published 2017 by
Newcastle Centre for the Literary Arts,
Newcastle University,
Newcastle upon Tyne NE1 7RU,
in association with
Bloodaxe Books Ltd,
Eastburn,
South Park,
Hexham,
Northumberland NE46 1BS.

www.bloodaxebooks.com
For further information about Bloodaxe titles
please visit our website or write to
the above address for a catalogue.

Supported using public funding by

**ARTS COUNCIL
ENGLAND**

Printed in Great Britain by Bell & Bain Limited, Glasgow, Scotland, on
acid-free paper sourced from mills with FSC chain of custody certification.

NEWCASTLE/BLOODAXE POETRY SERIES: 16

ANNE STEVENSON:

ABOUT POEMS

NEWCASTLE/BLOODAXE POETRY SERIES

1: Linda Anderson & Jo Shapcott (eds.)
Elizabeth Bishop: Poet of the Periphery

2: David Constantine: *A Living Language*
NEWCASTLE / BLOODAXE POETRY LECTURES

3: Julia Darling & Cynthia Fuller (eds.)
The Poetry Cure

4: Jo Shapcott: *The Transformers*
NEWCASTLE / BLOODAXE POETRY LECTURES
[Delayed title: now due 2018]

5: Carol Rumens: *Self into Song*
NEWCASTLE / BLOODAXE POETRY LECTURES

6: Desmond Graham: *Making Poems and Their Meanings*
NEWCASTLE / BLOODAXE POETRY LECTURES

7: Jane Hirshfield: *Hiddenness, Uncertainty, Surprise*
NEWCASTLE / BLOODAXE POETRY LECTURES

8: Ruth Padel: *Silent Letters of the Alphabet*
NEWCASTLE / BLOODAXE POETRY LECTURES

9: George Szirtes: *Fortinbras at the Fishhouses*
NEWCASTLE / BLOODAXE POETRY LECTURES

10: Fiona Sampson: *Music Lessons*
NEWCASTLE / BLOODAXE POETRY LECTURES

11: Jackie Kay, James Procter & Gemma Robinson (eds.)
Out of Bounds: British Black & Asian Poets

12: Sean O'Brien: *Journeys to the Interior*
NEWCASTLE / BLOODAXE POETRY LECTURES

13: Paul Batchelor (ed.)
Reading Barry MacSweeney

14: John Halliday (ed.)
Don't Bring Me No Rocking Chair: poems on ageing

15: Gwyneth Lewis: *Quantum Poetics*
NEWCASTLE / BLOODAXE POETRY LECTURES

16: Anne Stevenson: *About Poems and how poems are not about*
NEWCASTLE / BLOODAXE POETRY LECTURES

To Neil Astley,
superb editor and friend of many years

Contents

This poem was first published in *The Hudson Review*, Vol. LXX,
No. 1 (Spring 2017)

How Poems Arrive

(to Dana Gioia)

You say them as your undertongue declares
Then let them knock about your upper mind
Until the shape of what they mean appears.

Like love, they're strongest when admitted blind,
Judging by feel, feeling with sharpened sense
While yet their need to be is undefined.

Inaccurate emotion – as intense
As action sponsored by adrenaline –
Feeds on itself, and in its own defence

Fancies its role humanitarian
But poems, butch or feminine, are vain
And draw their satisfactions from within,

Sporting with vowels, or showing off a chain
Of silver els and ms to host displays
Of intimacy or blame or joy or pain.

The ways of words are tight and selfish ways,
And each one wants a slot to suit its weight.
Lines needn't scan like this with every phrase,

But something like a pulse must integrate
The noise a poem makes with its invention.
Otherwise, write prose. Or simply wait

Till it arrives and tells you its intention.

Introduction

Between 23 February and 2 March 2016, I travelled the few miles from my home in Durham in the north-east of England to give the three annual Newcastle/Bloodaxe Poetry Lectures to a warm, attentive audience at Newcastle University. The working title of the lectures was *We thought we were living now, but we were living then*, from my poem 'The Fiction Makers', but I asked Neil Astley to publish them under a heading that emerged as a recurring theme as I wrote: *ABOUT POEMS and how poems are not about.*

The new title developed from an idea Wallace Stevens put forward in his book on the poetic imagination, *The Necessary Angel*. It was Stevens' perception that poetry differs from prose in being more than *about* a subject. Poetry is made of words, Stevens argued, and words above everything else in poetry are sounds. Robert Frost, though a self-declared opponent of modernism, in his own way had earlier come close to the same conclusion: poems for Frost were the sounds or cadences of a voice speaking, the *sound*, in other words, of sense. Neither view, of course, is definitive or final; many familiar poems can be identified by their subject matter. And verse is often no more than a mnemonic crutch. But it's been a hundred years since the so-called modernists crashed through the long-established rules of English verse, and I suspect the widespread popularity of "free", do-it-yourself poetry today has arisen at least partly as a reaction to the high-minded élitism of poets like Stevens and T.S. Eliot. It is surely a good thing, too, that poetry is no longer solely the prized possession of specialists – of teachers, academics, professional poets and literary critics; as it is also a good thing that a number of famous poems by dead men (rarely women) are no longer looked up to as the only definitive models. Poems, the populist argument runs, can and should be written by anyone and everyone who cares to communicate their feelings. What are words *for* if they are not *about* what they say?

Yet, without opposing today's democratisation of poetry, and while approving wholeheartedly of what one might call the psychotherapy of engaging with emotive language, in these lectures I have cited Stevens among other major 20th-century figures to put a case for the opposition. Poetry is for me primarily an art form in which words signify feelings and impressions that are not translatable out of the words and cadences in which they appear. Poems first began to be sung or spoken in conjunction with music and dance; writing them down was a much later development. And yet, as a dance only exists when it is performed, so a poem, like a song, exists only when it is heard and understood as a voice. In other words, to write a poem is to *hear* it as it forms in the mind, and then to feel out sounds and rhythms that one hopes will convey its sense to listeners and readers. All writers of course, listen to what they write, striving to convey meanings and feelings in recognisable sequences of words. But most writers of prose, whether of fiction or philosophy, rely on a shared understanding not only of words but of grammatical habits and expected patterns of expression. Poets (and a few poet-like authors: Laurence Sterne, James Joyce, Virginia Woolf) are apt to discover that what they decide to express is not everything their poems say. The words take over, arrive from parts of their minds they can't explain, take them by surprise, take dictation from subconscious experience, appear to them in dreams. In this respect, some poetry – I would say the best of it – is like music; it is certainly no easier to pin down with an adjective or two.

Of course, words are not only sounds. As was made so much of by literary critics towards the end of the last century, words are also "signifiers", symbols, pointers to objects, ideas, feelings, proofs, which all language (including that of music and mathematics) exists to exemplify. Indeed, language, in its immense variety, relates to reality in so many ways that philosophers are not likely soon to be out of business. Painters and visual artists are like musicians, working with non-verbal signifiers, creating images to impress the human eye as poets and composers create sound-patterns for the ear. What all the arts provide and have long provided can be best understood by calling on Wallace Stevens' favoured word *imagination* – that common human factor that makes us unique among the animals, through which our minds are able to communicate and please each other beyond the claims of instinct or of the immediate moment. Art and religion, story and myth, vision and aspiration, and indeed mathematical proof and technological invention would have no existence if it were not for human imagination, source of all our creativity. Yet despite today's ever more wonderful (and terrifying) technological advances, we are still banished, like Adam and Eve, from any certainty of a social or personal paradise. Outside every Eden of imagined perfection lies the reality of our animal life – Eliot's 'birth, copulation and death', the truths, falsehoods and social complexities of the actual world we know, test and share through our sense experience and wilful, speculative minds every day.

It is too easy today to hive off creative imagination in the arts from the investigative imagination that has given rise to so many new technologies; and since technology is so much in the ascendant, imaginative writing tends to be on the defensive. One can see why so many professional postmodernist writers and critics have tried to justify their theories by hiding them beneath a veneer of pseudo-scientific definitions; and why it should seem so important to some poets to 'make it new' at all costs. My own view – or rather the urgent feeling that has motivated these lectures – is that the widening gap between today's ambitious poetic innovators and the hundreds and thousands of eager amateurs who write poetry without having read anything much but the efforts of their fellow writing students is aesthetically unhealthy. I have tried, though, not to make too much of aesthetic disagreements but to focus instead on the many-faceted nature of imagination itself, which of course must be judged good or evil, life enhancing or destructive, according to its value as a human asset. In itself, imagination is neutral. Since my subject is poetry, I have singled out poets whose rhythmic vision and order of words I have found inspiring, W.B. Yeats, W.H. Auden, Robert Frost, Elizabeth Bishop. I wouldn't hesitate before putting William Shakespeare in the same bracket. In a similar group but perhaps labelled poets of faith, I would certainly include George Herbert, Gerard Manley Hopkins, Emily Dickinson, T.S. Eliot; and then, in a variation of that, Wallace Stevens for whom the 'Supreme Fiction' of poetry was a religion-without-a-God. I wonder if, in the same imaginative bracket, it wouldn't be fair to include Albert Einstein, Niels Bohr, or any living physicist working imaginatively today on quantum or string theory?

Meanwhile, whatever we call "truth" still remains dependent on perceived relationships between words or symbols. My contention in all three Bloodaxe lectures, is that the word 'imagination' means many things in many contexts, that 'making believe' is only one form of it, and that the insights of naturally curious, creative people – writers, artists, philosophers, scientists, alike – differ only in kind. We all draw upon different aspects of the imaginative faculty, which is as integral to the human mind as the circulation of the blood to the body. One might even argue that knowledge itself is imaginary, or at least that it is impossible to know anything without projecting the conclusions of our minds and senses on a "real world" that is part of us and yet always remains outside us. For what do we know, as many a philosopher has contended, that is not a process of our brains?

Keeping the limitations of all knowledge in mind, and given the difference between what a lively imagination concludes from observation, experience or hearsay and what it is able to project from its private or socially induced desires and will to believe, it is easy to understand Wallace Stevens' contention that language in poetry, as distinct from language in common use for communication, has its own sphere of meaning and relates only obliquely to the passing "facts" we witness in our daily lives. A poem, if it is to be a work of art, must reveal, like a piece of music or a painting, emotional elements conveyed by sounds, rhythms and references that are untranslatable into any other form of language. If it is to survive, a poem must be more than "about" a specific subject; it must be, in Stevens' term, abstract. It must be 'the cry of its occasion, / Part of the *res* [thing] itself and not about it'. This is not to say, as some language poets do, that words in a poem only relate to each other, but that in a poem, words are related by sounds and rhythmic patterns to shared feelings that are stronger and, in effect, aesthetically more meaningful (or, as some would say, more spiritual) than literal or dictionary meanings.

Another major theme of this year's lectures (the source of my original title) is that change is time's one permanently reliable condition, that it continually transforms the present into the past at the very moment it opens the future to further change. I argue that without an understanding of how poetry has re-invented itself throughout history, today's present innovations are likely to remain rootless and unnourished. Drawing on lines from my poem 'The Fiction Makers', I trace the principal theories, fashions and beliefs of modern poets in America and Britain from the nineteen thirties to the present (the span, in fact, of my own lifetime). Giving special attention to the voices of T.S. Eliot, Ezra Pound, William Carlos Williams, Denise Levertov, Richard Wilbur and Robert Lowell, I show how after World War II populist movements in the United States rose up against a university-based establishment, introducing a barbarian energy into the art while at the same time destroying its solid base in traditional rhythm and form. Each lecture features poets I consider to be among the most effective of their kind, ranging from W.B. Yeats and W.H. Auden to Frank O'Hara, John Ashbery, and Elizabeth Bishop. In my final lecture, I spoke of and quoted extensively from poet friends and contemporaries: G.F Dutton, Frances Horovitz and William Martin, finishing with a tribute to the voice and ear of Seamus Heaney.

The texts of the 2016 Newcastle/Bloodaxe Poetry Lectures stand somewhat apart from the texts of three additional talks given over the years at St Chad's College at the University of Durham. Like the Newcastle talks, these have mainly to do with

15

matters of language-patterns, sounds and rhythms, reflecting my own belief that the defining virtue of poetry is its imaginative commitment to expressing the most elusive and yet truthful aspects of what we feel; that the major poets of our time have been compelled by a special relationship with language to persist in expressing in their poetry a central meaning for their lives – which by some miracle of understanding also affects the lives of their admirers. As a final chapter, having had a number of second thoughts about *Bitter Fame*, my biography of Sylvia Plath written in the 1980s, I conclude with a talk presented at the Ledbury Poetry Festival in 2013, which reassesses the work of this tragically gifted young American who was, strange to think of, born only two months or so before I was.

Poems for the Voice and Ear

Let me begin by quoting a passage from the Czech-French novelist Milan Kundera's *The Art of the Novel*, written in the long-ago 1980s.

There would seem to be nothing more obvious, more tangible and palpable than the present moment. And yet it eludes us completely. All the sadness of life lies in that fact. In the course of a single second, our sense of sight, of hearing, of smell, register (knowingly or not) a swarm of events, and a parade of sensations and ideas passes through our heads. Each instant represents a little universe, irrevocably forgotten in the next instant.[1]

An intriguing idea, bordering cleverly on the romantic from the author of *The Unbearable Lightness of Being*, and like the French existential philosophers, Kundera seems to have hit on a partial truth – a grain of truth, perhaps, wrapped in impressive-sounding layers of exaggeration. For in claiming that 'each instant represents a little universe irrevocably forgotten in the next instant' he has left out the element of memory, the thread of continuous consciousness that we take for granted as second passes into second, and yet we remain, for the most part, secure in the sense of ourselves, capable of looking back and looking forward as we experience, without thinking, the events of every day. Human memory is, on one hand, a kind of automatic motor that keeps us going through the years, and on another, what we might call a higher, repeatable form of experience that preserves our impressions and ideas in writing or music or painting. If it were true, as Kundera asserts, that the present moment always eludes us completely, we would all be suffering all the time from Alzheimer's.

Nevertheless, the kernel of truth in Kundera's contention, if not the cause of all the sadness of life, can hardly be dismissed as a mere philosophic attitude. Time does pass, memory is necessarily selective, much is lost, and it is true that in the 20th century, thanks to Freud and psychoanalysis, we became aware of how much our memories are at the mercy of chance, of will, of imagination, of dreams – aware, in short, of how much we lose of life as we live it. I say this as a kind of warning because these lectures have, for the most part, been dug out of layers of my memory. As I look back over the decades I have lived through and the poems I have written along the way, I am conscious of how many of them concern themselves with time, with how our minutes disappear (*Minute by Glass Minute*) and become, if not forgotten, creations of imagination rather than of fact or truth.

I will start by reading the poem that gave me my first title for these lectures. It was written in 1983 in memory of the poet Frances Horovitz who died that year at the heartbreaking age of 45. I thought at the time the poem was a celebration, a glance back at notable writers who had predeceased her and still remain in the memories of us all. Today, it seems to me more of a lament, a reflection on the futility of writing as time passes like a juggernaut over the names and hopes of 20th-century literary figures. In the order they appear the poem names Hemingway, Ezra Pound, Virginia Woolf, Lytton Strachey, Auden, Isherwood, Dylan Thomas, Sylvia Plath (a golden lotus planted among fierce flames), John Berryman (with his ironic doubles, Henry and Mr Bones), and finally Frances herself.

The Fiction Makers

We were the wrecked elect,
the ruined few. Youth,
youth, the Café Iruña
and the bullfight set,
looped on Lepanto brandy
but talking 'truth'.
Hem, the 4 a.m. wisecrack,
the hard way in,

that story we were all at the end of
and couldn't begin –
we thought we were living now,
but we were living then.

Sanctified Pound, a knot
of nerves in his fist,
squeezing the Goddamn iamb
out of our verse,
making it new in his
archaeological plot –
to maintain 'the sublime'
in the factive? Couldn't be done.
Something went wrong
with 'new' in the Pisan pen;
he thought he was making now,
but he was making then.

Virginia, Vanessa,
a teapot, a Fitzroy fuss,
'Semen?' asked Lytton,
eyeing a smudge on a dress.
How to educate England
and keep a correct address
on the path to the river through
Auschwitz? Belsen?
Auden and Isherwood
stalking glad boys in Berlin –
they thought they were suffering now,
but they were suffering then.

Pink-cheeked from Cwmdonkin,
Dylan with his Soho grin.
Planted in the fiercest of flames,
gold ash on a stem.
When Henry jumped out of his joke,
Mr Bones sat in.
Even you, with your breakable heart
in your ruined skin,
those poems all written
that have to be you, dear friend,
you guessed you were dying now,
but you were dying then.

19

Here is a table with glasses,
ribbed cages tipped back,
or turned on a hinge to each other
to talk, to talk,
mouths that are drinking or smiling
or quoting some book,
or laughing out laughter as candletongues
lick at the dark.
So bright in this fiction
forever becoming its end,
we think we are laughing now,
but we are laughing then.

Not after all, a poem that asserts that literature outlasts life
and is worth suffering for; rather a reminder that we never know
the full meaning of what we write; the present never lasts; time
passes, and just as what happened in the past was, while it was
happening, the present, so what is happening now in our present
present will in years to come be thought of as the past. Looking
at this poem, though, from the point of view of our present
present, I see that in contrasting the words 'now' and 'then' in
a repeated refrain I wasn't sufficiently conscious that the word
'then' in English refers both to the past and to the future. When
we say casually, I'll see you tomorrow; I'll see you *then*, 'then'
is a word that anticipates a time to come. (This excludes a third
use of 'then' in *if-then* clauses, such as *if* you invite me, *then*
I'll come.) It's tempting to treat such a slippery time-term
lightly, though I doubt that T.S. Eliot felt disposed to joke
when penning the opening lines of *Four Quartets*. My poem,
although it owes a good deal to Eliot's, is certainly not suggesting
that time is eternally present or that it's irredeemable. The
jaunty tone and music of 'The Fiction Makers' contradict its
sombre message; besides, the poem hides a paradoxical time
dimension that later crept up and surprised me. Nothing in my
experience is more important about the writing of poems than
that they should surprise you; that while you are submitting to
their rigorous demands of rhythms and sounds they find a way
of saying things you never meant to say or never knew you knew.
Prose is more practical, yet any creative language is, or should

be, an invitation to discovery. Although I have written poems all my life, as a student at the University of Michigan in the early 1950s, I adopted the superior, ignorant, utterly mistaken attitude of someone who already "knew" English literature and avoided the English programme as much as I could. I studied music for two years and then, under the sway of T.S. Eliot and Eliot's enthusiasm for Dante, picked up what I could of Italian and French, but I was far too self-absorbed writing, acting, playing the cello and creating with my artist friends a modernism all of Michigan's own to apply my mind, as I now wish I had, to the roots of English in Latin and Greek. However, I was, I suppose, harmlessly ignorant. The narrow textual view of the so-called New Criticism dominated language teaching in the 1950s; and neither Postmodern Literary Theory nor Creative Writing had been heard of. Eight years later, as a graduate student, chastened and returned to the University, I was impressed by the criticism of I.A. Richards and William Empson, but it wasn't until I met the poet and critic Philip Hobsbaum in Glasgow in the 1970s that I began to care a great deal about the good and the bad – i.e. the rigorous and the lazy ways – poems can come into the world. Two critical studies I valued and – influenced by Hobsbaum – taught during the 70s and 80s remain on my bookshelves, neither of which, I suspect, is much consulted today. The first was a study published by Oxford University Press in 1962 called *Poetry and the Physical Voice* by a senior lecturer at the University of Sheffield, Francis Berry. The second was by an American academic, Louise Rosenblatt, who, out of the blue, sent me her thoughtful *The Reader, the Text, the Poem* when I was living in Langley Park, Durham, during the Thatcher years. I particularly want to express my debt to these critical studies because I suspect they have been overlooked during the shifts and changes that have taken place in literary fashion since they were published. So let me first briefly sketch out Louise Rosenblatt's central idea, which gives the reader, or rather a series of readers, a prominent role in the creation of a poem over time; then I will go on to consider the unique contribution of the poet's individual voice.

The 20th-century criticism Dr Rosenblatt and I absorbed in our years as American undergraduates was, as I have said, under the domination of the self-labelled New Critics who stressed the objectivity of texts over authors and discouraged biographical and emotionally impressionistic analyses; the poem was its text, and that was all. Dr Rosenblatt quietly shifted the spotlight away from fixed texts and focused it instead not even on the critic but on the reader.

> The poem must be thought of as an event in time. It is not an object or an ideal entity. A poem happens during a coming together [...] of a reader and a text. The reader brings to the text his past experience and present personality. Under the magnetism of the ordered symbols of the text, he marshals his resources and crystallises out from the stuff of memory, thought, and feeling a new order, a new experience, which he sees as the poem. This becomes part of the ongoing stream of his life experience, to be reflected on from any angle important to him as a human being.[2]

'This concept of the poem as an experience shaped by the reader under guidance of a text,' Rosenblatt continues, 'shocks those who assume that a name, a title, must point to a thing [...] an object. But when we think of what a title – *Hamlet*, say, or *Moby Dick* – might refer to apart from a reader [...] "the work" disappears. The title then refers to a set of black marks on ordered pages or to a set of sounds vibrating in the air.'[3] Rosenblatt's transactional theory, then, suggests that for classical as for modern texts there are no correct readings. Although a context needs to be shared, there is no such thing as a definitive meaning of a literary work but instead as many readings within range of it as there are readers – then and now, past, present and future. The analogy is with performance: every reader who interacts with a poem, play or novel in a sense decides how to perform it, as a musician performs a musical score. For where is the music if not in the order of sounds played or heard? Not, certainly, in the black dots the composer scatters over the staves.

Of course, attributing the affect of poetry to readers rather than to poets or texts begs the question of what constitutes a good or a bad reading. Readers who have no experience of the culture, ideas or feelings described will read without responding unless the text is explained. Nor is all written language literature; very little of it is, any more than all tones and pitches are music. We need to distinguish between cognitive language that identifies, solves problems or informs us, and emotive language that expresses human feelings and impressions. In days gone by philosophers were happy creaming off emotive from referential texts, but the metaphorical nature of all words and symbols enlarges the category of language beyond the range of easy definition. Here again, as Rosenblatt suggests, if we shift our focus of attention from texts to readers we will be in a better position to know why we read instructions for making a cake, for instance, or taking a medicine with different expectations than those we adopt when confronted with a work of imagination. To point up the differences between these two types of language, Rosenblatt distinguishes what she calls 'efferent' or informational reading from 'aesthetic' reading: 'efferent' from the Latin *efferre*, to carry away, and 'aesthetic', which despite a *fin de siècle* overhang from Walter Pater, derives from a Greek word meaning an appeal to the senses rather than to the mind. Poetry, of course, can appeal to the mind, the emotions and the senses, and in a good poem aesthetic and efferent language often work in tandem. A poet who relies exclusively on aesthetic language, like Swinburne, say, or some of our modern language poets, risks losing readers through affectation or obscurity. All the poets whose works we particularly value were surely readers or listeners before they were writers. Even today, for all our emphasis on creative writing and therapeutic self-expression, who would think of writing poems or stories who hadn't been first inspired by the poems and stories of predecessors? Even as readers of our own poems, we can be surprised by new insights, as I was by re-reading 'The Fiction Makers' and realising it implied a dimension of future time I hadn't taken into account before.

I will come back to Rosenblatt's 'transactional' theory and to the give and take between readers and literary texts, as also to her terms 'efferent' and 'aesthetic'. But now let's look at the poet's side of the creative equation via Frances Berry's investigations in *Poetry and the Physical Voice*. What do we mean when we speak of a poet's voice? Well, usually two things we shouldn't confuse. There is the physical voice, an *articulation*, either vocal or mental – a pattern of long or short, stressed or unstressed syllables as they come to mind in the course of writing a poem. Then there is a sense in which the phrase 'the poet's voice' is used metaphorically to refer to an individual's speech idiom or characteristic mode of expression. I am more interested in the physical noises out of which a poem is made. I assume (as Berry does not) that the noises a poet hears in his mind before writing them down are the same sounds he would make if he were to speak them aloud, yet like Berry I suspect that sound often comes *first* in a poem's inception; such, at least, as has been the experience of Tennyson, Hopkins, Yeats, Frost, Mandelstam – and myself. On these terms, of course, few among the world's writers are poets because if poetry is 'primarily sound and but secondarily meaning', a poet's determining characteristic is precisely this 'physical or passional awareness of vocal sound'. This is why form and subject matter 'are consequent rather than precedent'. The poet 'lives or endures' a series of sounds, which force from them (and from him) a 'seemingly simultaneous and yet really consequent semantic energy'.[4]

I wouldn't make so much of Francis Berry's probably forgotten study of the poet's voice if his evocation of a poet *enduring* a series of sounds, which *forces* a 'semantic energy' from the language had not struck me forcibly at a time when I was beginning to feel my way into what I thought poetry was or should be. Like Louise Rosenblatt, Ezra Pound and Wallace Stevens among others, Berry asserts, I think rightly, that in poetry language is not a means to an end but an end in itself. 'The language in the constitution of the poem *is* the experience.' The poet in writing, instead of telling us about an experience, creates it in the act of making the poem. 'And since poetry is of active language, which is vocal sound, the poet's sensation of language is a specifically intimate, passional, nervous and somatic (or bodily) one.'[5]

I am not talking here of the friendly workshop poetry that enthusiasts, gifted and ungifted, are producing and sharing in every corner of Britain today. A great deal of home made and internet poetry is, of course, about – and thrives on being about – almost anything that is happening anywhere in our dangerous and rapidly shrinking world. It's hardly surprising that poetry writing, like amateur painting, has become an intensely personal creative outlet for thousands who 50 years ago might have been happier as readers or reciters. Creative writing has emerged as one way in which individuals can establish identities for themselves in our ever more bureaucratic, technological, button-punching, screen-watching society of sharers and carers. It perhaps doesn't matter if the great mass of poetry produced today has little connection with what used to be a rare, specialised art of language. Any suggestion of mine or of aesthetically-minded critics that true poetry is not *about* anything but itself probably registers a complaint about declining standards. In a quasi-poem called '20–200 on 747' an American poet, Heather McHugh, impatiently puts down a questioner on an airplane.

> Given an airplane, chance
> encounters always ask, So what
> are your poems about? They're about
> their business, and their father's business, and their
> monkey's uncle, they're about
> how nothing is about, they're not
> about about...[6]

It's an answer that 'drives them/ back to the snack tray every time' but it doesn't explain why this poet edges away from explaining herself. Poetry, she says, could be as serious as young Jesus in the temple or as silly as talk of a monkey's uncle, but poems should not be put at the service of small talk or propaganda or issues better handled by 'efferent' prose. One understands her objection to shallow, sentimental thinking about poetry, but rudely to dismiss an innocent questioner verges on snobbery. How, in short, in this new century, which already feels as threatened and imperilled as the last one, can we make a case for W.H. Auden's famous lines in his elegy, 'In Memory of W.B. Yeats'?

> For poetry makes nothing happen: it survives
> In the valley of its saying where executives
> Would never want to tamper [...]
>   it survives,
> A way of happening, a mouth.[7]

To adequately defend Auden's view, I will have to cite one more literary critic, Angela Leighton, who in 2007 published *On Form*,[8] a book which laid out and analysed the development of aestheticism in poetry since Edwardian times, offering an explanation of Heather MacHugh's negative views of 'about' and augmenting it with appealing, and to me convincing, hints about the line, 'Poetry makes nothing happen.' Leighton suggests (and I have taken the idea further) that the potent word 'nothing' in English (see *King Lear*) can mean both *no thing* and *not one thing*. And *not one thing* can, of course, mean more than one thing, or many things. Since poetry is concerned to express feelings, and feelings cannot be pinned down in points a, b, c like logical ideas, 'nothing' in Auden's line could mean that poetry sets in motion not one mental happening but many. 'Poetry makes no thing happen' could refer to any number of emotional responses that continue to shimmer beyond the life times of both poet and readers. Neither a thing nor a no thing, Yeats' poetry, like that of every memorable poet, is a kind of unfinished speaking, sound-patterns that run on through time, surviving the dead poet's 'mouth' and 'way of happening' in the remembered body of his words and cadences that, as Auden says, are now 'scattered among a hundred cities / And wholly given over to unfamiliar affections'.[9]

Later on, in the same chapter, Leighton comes up with an analysis of Yeats' extraordinary sense of rhythm as the source of this 'unfinished speaking'. For though Yeats claimed to be

26

tone deaf, in the few recording that exist of his readings, we hear him chanting his poems; even without such evidence, it would be difficult to disagree that it was through the music of his rhythms and the sonority of his rhymes, and not through his politics or philosophy, that Yeats achieved greatness as a poet. Here again, we see the dimensions, oral and rhythmic, of a poet's voice taking precedence over his ideas. Yeats's mythological beliefs, his visions, his gyres and phases of the moon, his personal love affairs and Irish politics are all raised to the highest plane of art by the vocal noises his poems make and by the counterpoint of rhythm against metre in his lines. 'Footbeats for the metre and heartbeats for the rhythm' wrote Robert Frost, who in his American idiom was both a defender and a master of vocal effects. 'Poetry plays the rhythms against a grid of meter.' And no poet has ever done so more effectively that W.B. Yeats. Listen to the hexameters of 'The Magi', its 12 or 13 syllables per line broken into patches of sound governed by vowel length. (And, by the way, if I suggest that this poem is not 'about' the Magi, I don't mean that it has no subject. In the Christian-based culture we share, we all know the story, but I wouldn't say Yeats's poem is 'about' that story. It is based on it; it refers to it, but it suggests many levels of human 'searching', of looking for an answer.)

> Now   as at **all times**   I can **see**   in the **mind's eye**,
> In their **stiff, painted clothes**,   the **pale** unsatisfied **ones**
> **Appear** and **dis**appear   in the **blue depth** of the **sky**.
> With **all** their **ancient faces**   like **rain**-beaten **stones**,
> And **all** their **helms** of **silver**   hovering **side** by **side**,
> And **all** their **eyes still fixed**,   hoping to **find once more**,
>   [-/ -/ // /- -/ //]
> Being by **C**alvary's **tur**bulence unsatisfied,   [/- -/- -/- - -/- -]
> The **un**controllable **mys**tery on the **bestial floor.**[11]

Unless a reader gives full measure to the long plodding vowels of 'all' and 'eye', 'pale' and 'ones, as to the repeated 'all' of the middle lines, imitating the pace of the Magi themselves as they plod towards Bethlehem (in 'eyes still fixed' and 'find once more' each word wants a stress) the poem will flow too swiftly to the penultimate line, where a quickening pace of multi-syllable words introduced the rushed, almost panicking 13 syllables of the final line. The reader has to decide whether to lengthen the pause between 'mystery' and 'on' in the last line or to give 'on' a stress to fill out the hexameter's six accents. I personally would lengthen the pause to give emphasis to the word 'mystery' – pronounced in two syllables, as also, 'bestial'.

Yeats' lyrics with their repeated choruses and mythological references are even further removed from anything that is being said about anything. If there is a personal or political intent hidden within the ballad-like 'I am of Ireland', it is hardly relevant to the stanza Yeats borrowed from a 14th-century lyric:

> '*I am of Ireland,*
> *And the Holy Land of Ireland,*
> *And time runs on,' cried she.*
> '*Come out of charity,*
> *Come dance with me in Ireland.'*

It would be crude, surely, to claim that this song is 'about' Ireland. The female speaker is more a visionary spirit than the personification of an actual country, an idealised figure who sings on regardless of the 'one man alone' who turns 'his stately head' and objects. Does it matter who or what this sceptical man represents in the Ireland of Yeats' imagination? Or if the 'out-landish band' he so roundly abuses is a metaphor for Ireland's political incompetence?

> 'The fiddlers are all thumbs,
> Or the fiddle-string accursed,
> The drums and the kettledrums
> And the trumpets all are burst,
> And the trombone,' cried he,
> 'The trumpet and the trombone,'
> And cocked a malicious eye [...]'[12]

The poem is a fairy tale, complete with fairy queen and grumbling ogre, and its import is that of a make-believe enchantment summoned to relieve the dismal truths of reality. The same can be said of most of Yeats's song-like refrains:

> *I carry the sun in a golden cup,*
> *The moon in a silver bag.*[13]

or

> *Like a long-legged fly upon the stream,*
> *His mind moves upon silence.*[14]

Even in poems that resonate philosophically or psychologically, Yeats's powerful rhymes and rhythmic pulse carry his lines straight into a reader's mind and memory.

> [*regular 4 stress iambics until final line*]
> Everything that man esteems
> Endures a moment or a day.
> Love's pleasure drives his love away,
> The painter's brush consumes his dreams;
> The herald's cry, the soldier's tread
> Exhaust his glory and his might:
> Whatever flames upon the night
> Man's own resinous heart has fed.[15]
> [/ / /- -/ - / – *final line opens with 3 adjacent stresses*]

My own debt to Yeats' rhythms, I confess, is very great, and because of this I'm inclined slightly to revise Francis Berry's theory and suggest that an 'ear' rather than a voice is the primary organ needful to a young poet beginning to listen out for poems to learn from.

Now, I going to digress from critical generalisations and take up an example of an initiation into poetry with which I am more familiar than any other – my own. Like everyone impelled to write poetry I was the unwitting pupil of the aural environment of my upbringing, and I was lucky. My American parents were not only readers; they were readers aloud. Poetry was drummed into my ears from my earliest years: nursery rhymes, folksongs and song-games, music to play and to dance to, poems to learn by heart and recite at school assemblies. My family's readings aloud of Shakespeare's plays and my father's sonorous renditions of Walter Scott, Wordsworth, Browning, Matthew Arnold and yes, plenty of Yeats, drilled classical English metres into me before I knew what an iamb was or what poets had to teach me beyond nature worship and some heroic tales of derring-do. I have already mentioned the disadvantages of such an early introduction to English verse. By the time I got to university I'd decided, quite wrongly, that I knew English literature too well and loved it too much to spoil it by study. So I majored in music, and then fled to England, married, failed to become a cellist or a schoolteacher or even a wife and returned to Ann Arbor, Michigan with a three-year old daughter to become a student again. The year was 1960, and I was in luck when one of my professors, the poet, Donald Hall, asked me to show him some poems. I said I had none to show him. 'Well,' he said, 'then you must have some to write.' How did he know? It had never occurred to me that just sitting down pen in hand might bring poems to my head. But, of course, there were plenty to write. My mother was dying of cancer; my father was not finding much consolation in philosophy, I was home again, a stranger in my hometown. So I began to write a poem called 'Ann Arbor', the first of a series Hall half praised, half criticised (too 'Auden-esque', he said) that eventually went into a first collection, *Living in America*, in 1966.

Now it happened that in 1957, Donald Hall, after a fellow-ship year at Oxford, had been one of three editors of a popular anthology called *The New Poets of England and America*,[16] published in paperback in New York, with an introduction by Robert Frost, containing poems by 52 young poets aged 40 or under, many of whom had returned to university on the G.I. Bill after serving in the Armed Forces during the war. The names in the Table of Contents read today like candidates for a 20th-century Hall of Fame: among the Americans, Robert Lowell, Richard Wilbur, Anthony Hecht, Howard Nemerov, Louis Simpson; among the English, Philip Larkin, Geoffrey Hill, Thom Gunn, John Heath-Stubbs, Jon Silkin. Few women were admitted. Adrienne Cecile Rich and Elizabeth Jennings were allowed in, but in 1957 Elizabeth Bishop would have been

46, too old for the age limit, and Sylvia Plath and Anne Sexton were as yet unheard of. Two of the editors' *Second Selection*, published in 1962, found space for poems by both Plath and Sexton, as also by Ted Hughes and Denise Levertov; I will have more to say about Levertov in my second lecture. As for the diversity, quality and general good taste of the 1957 edition, it took its tone and colour smoothly from Robert Frost, who concluded his Introduction with a peon of praise for academia that – for a poet who never completed a college education – he seems to have been in two minds about himself.

> As I often say a thousand, two thousand, colleges, town and gown together in the little town they make, give us the best audiences for poetry ever had in this world. I am in on the ambition that this book will get to them – heart and mind.[17]

How vividly I remember that *New Poets* anthology resonating in my heart and mind as I began to write poetry in the early 1960s. At the time, the new poets who impressed me most were Donald Hall himself, who apart from setting me an example, earned my eternal gratitude by introducing me to the poetry of Elizabeth Bishop and then finding me a commission to write a book on her, and Richard Wilbur, whose formal elegance and wit set the tone for the entire volume. In view of the turbulent developments in American poetry in the later 1960s, it's important to realise that the formal standards set for readers and writers by Wilbur and his like were, in most university English Departments, accepted unquestionably as patterns for the future. Lines like these, for instance:

> Haze, char and the weather of All Souls';
> A giant absence mopes upon the trees:
> Leaves cast in casual potpourris
> Whisper their scents from pits and cellar holes.[18]

or these,

> The eyes open to a cry of pulleys,
> And spirited from sleep, the astounded soul
> Hangs for a moment bodiless and simple

As false dawn.
                    Outside the open window
The morning air is all awash with angels.[19]

Richard Wilbur's beautiful poetry – and it *is* beautiful, every word, every stress, every vowel and consonant perfectly placed – has always been something of a puzzle, because, although always admired, it has never, at least to my knowledge, been accounted 'major'. 'Clever', 'very good', 'perfect', 'delightful', 'charming' are epithets that have seemed appropriate, but not 'great', a term readily accorded to the poetry of Yeats and Eliot and, by many, to Frost and Stevens. Why? Leafing through the first *New Poets* anthology, I recently found myself lingering over fine passages of verse by Richard Wilbur, as also over powerful lines by the young Robert Lowell, yet finding something missing in their work. Wilbur's charm is infectious, but it is somehow too smooth, as if he could imitate 17th-century metaphysical poetry better than the Metaphysicals could write it themselves. Nothing is smooth or charming about Lowell's clenched descriptions of drowned sailors, adulterous marriages and ode-like invocations of sinners suffering in Hell. The young Lowell was a poet who needed to satisfy his ambition by writing lines that through their oceanic force would prove his major status. It was a source of torment to him that he trod in the footsteps of Hawthorne and Melville. A reader feels the effort put into every carefully rhymed end line of 'Mr Edwards and the Spider':

> On Windsor March, I saw the spider die
> When thrown into the bowels of fierce fire:
>   There's no long struggle, no desire
>   To get up on its feet and fly –
>   It stretches out its feet
> And dies. This is the sinner's last retreat;
> Yes, and no strength exerted on the heat
> Then sinews the abolished will, when sick
> And full of burning, it will whistle on a brick
>
> But who can plumb the sinking of that soul?
>   Josiah Hawley, picture yourself cast

> Into a brick-kiln where the blast
> Fans your quick vitals to a coal –
>   If measured by a glass,
> How long would it seem burning! Let there pass
> A minute, ten, ten trillion; but the blaze
> Is infinite, eternal; this is death.
> To die and know it. This is the Black Widow, death.[20]

Is that mere rhetoric? All those rhyming evocations of eternal pain attributed to the 17th-century hellfire preacher Jonathan Edwards – don't they in some way refer to more personal burnings of conscience and guilt, to the suffering of the poet's ambitious soul, maybe, in terror of being condemned by Freud for its sick life, and instead of being eternally burned in Hell, punished by being eternally forgotten? Compare Lowell's soul with Wilbur's as it wakes to watch a host of freshly washed angels dancing on a line outside his window.

> Some are in bed-sheets, some are in blouses,
> Some are in smocks: but truly there they are.
> Now they are rising together in calm swells
> Of halcyon feeling, filling whatever they wear
> With the deep joy of their impersonal breathing [...] [21]

The significant line there is 'With the deep joy of their impersonal breathing', absolving the poet from self-consciousness as from Freudian hang-ups. The soul that is about to descend to 'the punctual rape of every blessed day' has been washed clean of it sins as it wittily pleads, 'Oh, let there be nothing on earth but laundry, / Nothing but rosy hands in the rising steam/ and clear dances done in the sight of heaven.' Lowell wished, too, to be freed from his own personality, but it's as if he rarely was able to release himself from a sense of sin. Even in 'Waking Early Sunday Morning' (written in the 1960s) he breaks 'loose, like the Chinook/ salmon' in the first stanza, only to feel 'the unpolluted joy/ and criminal leisure of a boy...' And by the end of a long, unsettling meditation on (or about) the political doldrums of his time, he moralises, almost awkwardly,

Pity the planet, all joy gone
from this sweet volcanic cone;
peace to our children when they fall
in small war on the heels of small
war – until the end of time
to police the earth, a ghost
orbiting forever lost
in our monotonous sublime.[22]

In contrast, Wilbur's waking soul descending 'in bitter love' to accept his body, is happy to become no more than a man welcoming a physical world in which everyone, from thieves to lovers to nuns, looks to be 'washed clean'.

'Bring them down from their ruddy gallows;
Let there be clean linen for the backs of thieves;
Let lovers go fresh and sweet to be undone,
And the heaviest nuns walk in a pure floating
Of dark habits,
            keeping their difficult balance.'[23]

Both 'Waking Early Sunday Morning' and 'Love Calls Us to the Things of This World' seem to me fine poems, typical of their time and place. Wilbur has never written a better one; Lowell's is more uneven, but has wonderful moments. Yet I would like to leave you to consider that both these poets, along with most of those represented by the 1957 edition of *New Poets of England and America* were writing at the end of a tradition, not at the beginning of one. Robert Lowell, Richard Wilbur, Donald Hall, Elizabeth Bishop – all models to me – were practitioners of a poetry of the voice and ear, fundamental to the art since the Elizabethans, and before. The same iambic line, the musical cadence, the memorable alliteration and assonance of verbal noises can be heard, refreshed but not greatly altered, in the poetry of Yeats, Auden, Wallace Stevens and Robert Frost and are patterns overheard in (or underlying) the rhythms of Eliot's *The Waste Land* as in Ezra Pound's *Cantos*. Francis Berry considered that anything differing in respect to form and sound could not be poetry. Louise Rosenblatt believed that teaching students to read poetry necessarily involved hearing it as well as recreating it. Only as recently, I would guess, as the 1990s in Britain, has a revolution in education, media technology and egalitarian idealism brought about a state of affairs in which anything "new" and in "free verse" that breaks with academia can be called poetry. And this suggests, despite cult figures such as Seamus Heaney and recently Elizabeth Bishop, that poets are not so special after all. A culture of literary festivals, creative writing groups and poetry competitions has grown up in the past 20 or 30 years in which almost everyone who acknowledges deep feelings is encouraged to express them. It seems to me both a good and a bad thing that in Britain today anyone who really wishes to be considered a poet is welcome to throw his or her hat in the ring and try for a large monetary prize.

Next week I will focus on how a truly popular poetry rose in the United States out of the depression, the Second World War and a particularly American dislike of eggheads. It is not my purpose to take sides in what for so many years of the mid 20th century featured as a war between university palefaces and revolutionary redskins. What does seem clear is that by 1957 something about Robert Frost's thousands of university and college communities of poets had to change. There was simply too much umpty-umpty iambic rhyming around to catch the hearts of a population under the rhythmic sway of Frank Sinatra and Elvis Presley. Perhaps the lesson of that time was that poetry cannot and should not always expect to be great art. Eliot, Pound and the modernists laid down the law too rigorously. The notion that poetry has to be difficult does not seem to have affected the popularity of Chaucer or Shakespeare (in their private lives, a business man and an actor), and although individual geniuses throughout the ages have been recognised and honoured, the sheer multiplicity of poets competing for publishers or prizes in recent years has necessarily lowered the oral and aural standards of the art even as our celebrity-mad society hypes more and more individual names. Whether a poem was great, good or indifferent used to be a matter for readers with different tastes in different times to decide. But if poetry is to be written in the future, some kind of continuity with the voices and ears of the past will have to be maintained. And that will be a matter to settle not by those who are living 'now' but by whomever will be debating poetry 'then'. I suggest we leave that particular 'then' at least until tomorrow.

Thank you all very much for listening to me tonight.

The Anthology as Manifesto 1960-1980

We are living our whole lives in a state of emergency.
DENISE LEVERTOV, 1967

In the first of these lectures I introduced the idea of the poem
as an enduring event rather than a literary object, drawing
attention to the American critic Louise Rosenblatt's 'transactional
theory of the literary work' in which the reader interacting with
the text undertakes a creative role in keeping a poem alive.
Next I pointed out that, since poets are themselves readers, a
poem rarely starts from scratch, that there are noises, rhythms,
cadences echoing in a poet's ear, even if unconsciously exper-
ienced; that the impulse to say or sing or write a poem usually
has an origin in other poems remembered and admired. I spoke
of poems– or the best, most memorable poems – as being exper-
iences in themselves rather than about experience, drawing
examples from Yeats and Auden before going on to cite Hall,
Pack and Simpson's 1957 anthology, *New Poets of England and
America*, as an example of the Anglo-American tradition to
which I felt I belonged when I started to write poems myself.
Towards the end I asked you to read with me two poems from
this anthology that I considered "good", though perhaps not
"great": Richard Wilbur's 'Love Calls Us to the Things of this
World' and Robert Lowell's 'Mr Edwards and the Spider'. I
asked you to consider whether these poems suffered, for all
their excellence of form and language, from being written
towards the end of a tradition. Is it not inevitable that once a
style has been achieved and a technique developed – in any art
– that, as Yeats eloquently put it, 'Everything that man esteems/
[...] Exhausts his glory and his might'; that however bright the

37

flame of inspiration burns, it eventually wears out the generations that nourished it.

'Make it new,' Ezra Pound demanded in the early years of the last century, and sure enough in 1960, three years after Hall, Pack and Simpson's anthology, *New Poets of England and America* introduced a fresh generation of post-war poets to mid-century readers, a counter-anthology appeared from the University of California Press in Berkeley entitled *The New American Poetry*. Ignoring England as if its poetic tradition were poison, and choosing to represent a group of iconoclastic Americans scarcely heard of in American universities and colleges, an unknown editor, Donald Allen, brought out a collection of avant-garde voices that exploded in the literary atmosphere like the time bomb it was intended to be. Not one of the American names that had appeared in the Hall/Pack/Simpson anthology turned up in this one; not one among this even newer roster of American poets had merited so much as a mention in the former. The split right down the middle of the American poetic tradition was sudden, violent and absolute – a culture war that took itself immensely seriously and raged fiercely throughout the ensuing decades, with gender, racial and ideological permutations that have since affected the forms and reforms of poetry all over the world.

Needless to say, in the light of my enthusiasm for Donald Hall and his friends and in my excitement when I obtained, through Hall, a commission to write a first critical study of Elizabeth Bishop, I sided throughout the 60s and 70s with the university wits – with Philip Rahv's palefaces against the rebellious redskins, or in Robert Lowell's choice of epithets, I opted for cooked poetry over raw. Today, though, I am inclined to think the kind of shaking up the new American roughs gave to the palefaces, particularly in the 1960s, was a good thing. It broadened the reach and importance of poetry immensely; no longer could new American poetry pretend to be wholly the accomplishment of a few poets pampered by university English departments, in danger of trading their freedom to express and explore new forms for the safety of tenure. Donald Allen's terse

Preface to his new poets (hardly new today, of course) traced their heritage back to Ezra Pound – venerating him as their founding grandfather over the more anglicised T.S. Eliot – and then through William Carlos Williams (a big debt there), to sub-modernists like Wallace Stevens, Marianne Moore, E.E. Cummings, and to a mid-century generation that embraced, among others, Louis Zukofsky, Robert Duncan, John Berryman and Frank O'Hara. At root, however, the wild new poets of the 1960s stemmed from William Blake and Walt Whitman. They emerged, raging and full of theories, in Berkeley and San Francisco, Boston, New York City and conspicuously in a small experimental arts college called Black Mountain in North Carolina. Different as these poets were as to aim and origin, they shared one common characteristic: 'a total rejection of all those qualities typical of academic verse'.[1] It seemed not to affect this 'total rejection', either, that many of them who, after the war, were inspired to create anti-academic poetry on the model of Pound and Williams had discovered their vocations while benefiting from the G.I. Bill and studying as mature students in universities across America. Older than their student peers, war-hardened, disgusted with middle-class smugness and feeling superior to their professors, they were ready enough to throw away in scorn what seemed to them the same tired, outmoded systems of metrics and versification that Pound had found objectionable in Georgian poetry 40 or 50 years earlier. What was to take the place of traditional verse, as likewise of traditional values, was a revolutionary art form closely allied to New Orleans jazz and to expressionist painting as it spread from avant-garde movements in France and Germany to New York and San Francisco.

Donald Allen, claiming (in 1960) that the new American poetry would become the dominant movement in the literature of the later 20th century, divided his poets into five groups, admittedly 'somewhat arbitrary', he wrote, yet useful in showing the range and variety of their work. The first group, in many ways a seed group, had been for years associated with Black Mountain College [2] and was composed of poets on its teaching staff and their students – Charles Olson, Robert Duncan, Robert Creeley, Edward Dorn – who were also founders and editors of two small magazines, *Origin* and *Black Mountain Review*. Among the poets discovered and published by *Black Mountain Review* was a young woman, a Welsh-English-Russian Jewish émigrée named Denise Levertov, married to an American and living in New York, about whose work I will have more to say later.

In the late 1940s, Black Mountain's Robert Duncan, dynamic and persuasive, moved to San Francisco to become a leading member of the anthology's second group. With Robin Blaser and, rather surprisingly, a Scottish woman ballad-maker, Helen Adam, he joined Jack Spicer in Berkeley to set a new trend in public poetry readings in the Bay Area. Lawrence Ferlinghetti's performances with jazz bands became famously popular, drawing huge crowds of students who in the mid 60s became the core of notorious uprisings against any and every manifestation of oppressive authority. By 1955, the anthology's third group, the self-named Beat Generation invented by Allen Ginsberg and Jack Kerouac, had likewise transferred their sphere of activity from New York to San Francisco, leaving a fourth group, initiated by John Ashbery, Kenneth Koch and Frank O'Hara, to found The New York School associated with such painters as Mark Rothko, Jackson Pollock, and (from Black Mountain again) Willem de Kooning – a group that in the 1960s turned the studios of New York's SoHo district into a vibrant centre of abstract art.

A fifth and younger group, under the influence of Gary Snyder and Philip Whalen from Reed College in Oregon, reached out across the continent to John Wieners in Boston, developing contingently yet independently of the San Francisco 'Beats'. It was this group that eventually attracted Lee Harwood and other radical young English poets to the American scene in a network of intense personal relationships that owed much to John Ashbery and Robert Creeley. In fact the 1999 reprint of the 1960 California anthology (in which no English poet is represented) looks to be nothing like the single-sided argument for American counter-culture poetics it later was reputed to be. As in the case of the more respectable Hall/Pack/Simpson anthology, Donald Allen's new poets had individual voices and wrote out of diverse backgrounds and beliefs, but because so many of them undertook to pronounce in the manner of Ezra Pound's *Cantos* upon the horrors of the 20th century, on madness, mythology, psychedelic trips, Eastern mystic philosophy and the evils of war (the Vietnam War, offshoot of the Cold War, already loomed large) their poems don't easily yield quotable or discussable passages. The opening lines of Ginsberg's *Howl* are typical – and famous:

> I saw the best minds of my generation destroyed by madness,
>   starving hysterical naked,
> dragging themselves through the negro streets at dawn looking
>   for an angry fix,
> angelheaded hipsters burning for the ancient heavenly connection
>   to the starry dynamo in the machinery of night,
> who poverty and tatters and hollow-eyed and high sat up smoking
>   in the supernatural darkness of cold-water flats floating
>   across the tops of cities contemplating jazz,
> who bared their brains to Heaven under the El and saw Moham-
>   medan angels staggering on the tenement roofs illuminated,
> who passed through universities with radiant cool eyes halluci-
>   nating Arkansas and Blake-light tragedy among the scholars
>   of war,
> who were expelled from the academies for crazy & publishing
>   obscene odes on the windows of the skull […] [3]

Read today in the light of today's futile wars in the Middle East, it's surprising to realise that Ginsberg wrote and published *Howl* as early as 1955-56. On the other hand, the witty and clever New York poet, Frank O'Hara, chose to tease his readers with long lines that embroider surreal effects out of images that lie quietly on the page until you realise how alarming they are – as in these opening lines of 'In Memory of My Feelings':

> My quietness has a man in it, he is transparent
> and he carries me quietly, like a gondola, through the streets.
> He has several likenesses, like stars and years, like numerals.

My quietness has a number of naked selves,
so many pistols I have borrowed to protect myselves
from creatures who too readily recognise my weapons
and have murder in their heart! [4]

This obviously comes from a world of city fears and surreal impressions not unlike Elizabeth Bishop's in her (to me) more convincingly mysterious 'The Man-Moth'. O'Hara, though, was a champion ironist, and his witty poem, 'Why I Am Not a Painter' tells us more about the theory behind abstract art and painting than screeds of academic criticism. Interestingly, what O'Hara says about words confirms my own prejudice against 'about', though he purposely ignores considerations of sound. He had no use for verse, believing that poetry might just as well or even better be written in *careful and very calculated* prose.

Why I Am Not a Painter

I am not a painter. I am a poet.
Why? I think I would rather be
a painter, but I am not. Well,

for instance, Mike Goldberg
is starting a painting. I drop in.
'Sit down and have a drink' he
says. I drink: we drink. I look
up. 'You have SARDINES in it.'
'Yes, it needed something there.'
'Oh.' I go and the days go by
and I drop in again. The painting
is going on, and I go, and the days
go by. I drop in. The painting is
finished. 'Where's SARDINES?'
All that's left is just
letters, 'It was too much,' Mike says.

But me? One day I am thinking of
a color: orange. I write a line
about orange. Pretty soon it is a
whole page of words, not lines.
Then another page. There should be

so much more, not of orange, of
words, of how terrible orange is
and life. Days go by. It is even in
prose. I am a real poet. My poem
is finished and I haven't mentioned
orange yet. It's twelve poems, I call
it ORANGES. And one day in a gallery
I see Mike's painting called SARDINES.[5]

Despite O'Hara's witty iconoclasm and that of a few others, a common characteristic of the poets represented in Donald Allen's selection was the high degree of Freudian anxiety and self-preoccupied "madness" that spread through American poetry after Robert Lowell (honoured by both schools) abandoned the mannered rhymes and forced couplets of his early books and, in *Life Studies*, relaxed into a style of prose-like personal narration. Early in 1959, Lowell's writing seminar at Boston University attracted both Anne Sexton and Sylvia Plath as students, but not Ted Hughes, who writing to Lucas Myers in England, deplored the self-interested individualism he detected everywhere in American society. This was well before the feminist movement of the 60s appropriated "confessional poetry" as the special province of women. 'It's a dangerous society,' wrote Hughes, 'that drives you to think your individuality is the only meaningful possession possible.'[6] And though Charles Olson was hardly a subscriber to Lowell's Bostonian guilt, his contributions to *The New American Poetry* were so packed with private references to William Carlos Williams and others among his heroes that the Black Mountain group was from the beginning regarded by poets such as Donald Hall, Richard Wilbur, Elizabeth Bishop and, indeed myself, as a clique of impenetrable mystifiers.

It could be that Olson's lasting contribution to Allen's anthology was never his 'Maximus Poems' but his *Statement on Poetics* in which he attempted to define and defend PROJECTIVE VERSE as opposed to what he called NON-PROJECTIVE or closed verse (the upper case letters are his own). PROJECTIVE OR OPEN VERSE (also labelled COMPOSITION BY FIELD) set out to oppose and replace the inherited line, stanza and overall form of 'old' verse. Olson didn't acknowledge that there are more forms than one of old verse. Nor was his claim to being original borne out by his demand that syllables not words be of primary 'use' in constructing a poem's lines. The poem itself, he argued, must, at all points, be 'a high energy construct… an energy-discharge' that passes 'the energy which propelled it in the first place' through 'the kinetics of the thing' to the reader. How? Well, he argues, once a field composition is launched in the open, the poem can continue by no track other than the one it declares for itself. Really? But isn't this what any good 'closed' poet would say – that a poem, once begun, flows on its own momentum of meaningful sounds and syllables? Has there ever existed a principle of English verse-making in which syll-ables have not been the fundamental units of sound? Syllables and vocal accents, not words, provide traditional stanzas with energy according to a rhythmic distribution of stresses, allowing for what has always been– except perhaps in the over rigorous 18th century – an extremely flexible set of English metrical rules. Olson refers approvingly to Pound's advice to compose in the sequence of the musical phrase, not of the metronome, before he provides, as an example of fine musical phrasing, this version of that most universally loved of English lyrics,

> O western wynd, when wilt thou blow
> And the small rain down shall rain,
> O Christ that my love were in my arms
> And I in my bed again. [7]

Another of Olson's upper-case pronouncements (this one cred-ited to Robert Creeley) is that 'FORM IS NEVER MORE THAN AN EXTENSION OF CONTENT', and here he does indeed reverse Francis Berry's contention, mentioned in my first lecture, that poetry is primarily sound and secondarily meaning conveyed through sound. And yet, whichever way around a poet thinks of how a voice, or as Olson insisted, 'breath', transmits syllabic energy through rhythmic lines to a listener or reader, it is a fact that in memorable poetry sound, rhythm and meaning are inseparable. So when Olson writes, boasting of his discovery that the poet composes his lines not out of feet and metre but out of syllables and breath,[8] I can't imagine Yeats or Eliot or Frost taking exception to anything but his uncomfortable wording. If there was anything new in Projective Verse, it probably was the freedom it granted to the poet to write all over the page, substituting gaps between broken lines and stanzas for standard punctuation. In which case, it is as well to recall Ezra Pound's strictures on vers libre in one of his earliest essays in *Pavannes and Divisions* (1918):

> Indeed *vers libre* has becomes as prolix and as verbose as any of the flaccid varieties that preceded it... The actual language and phrasing is often as bad as that of our elders without even the excuse that the words are shovelled in to fill a metric pattern or to complete the noise of a rhyme-sound...At times I can find a marked metre in 'vers libre' as stale and hackneyed as any pseudo-Swinburnian, at times the writers seem to follow no musical structure whatsoever.[9]

Whatever the philosophical pretensions and bullying principles of the Black Mountain poets, it was to Olson's credit that he, Duncan and Creeley, like Frank O'Hara and, yes, John Ashbery too, took their "alternative" poetry tremendously seriously as art. This might well have been true of the Beats, if their popularity hadn't brought them to the attention of all-American magazines like *Time* and *Life*, in which Ginsberg appeared glamourised as a new era prophet (as he believed himself to be) whose poems were news worthy not because of their quality as literature but because of his and Jack Kerouac's sensational public performances. Already in the 1950s, with the death of Dylan Thomas well in mind, elements of the American media were happy to portray poetry as a means of exploring new, preferably crazed types of consciousness, tempting the gullible young to participate in a flourishing (and delightfully illegal) psychedelic drug culture that masqueraded as a quest for Eastern mystical enlightenment.

I am looking back, now, not to the 1940s and 50s, when Donald Allen's alternative poets began to challenge the poetic tradition, but to those fraught and frustrating years of the 1960s/70s, amazed to think it must be 50 years since I observed the phenomenon of youthful hippies and flower people setting up campsites on the Commons of Boston and Cambridge in Massachusetts, dancing in Blake-like nightgowns or brewing cauldrons of brown rice to demonstrate not only and understandably against the Vietnam War and the technology of the industrial "system" but against any pressure from parents, teachers or persons in authority who appeared to thwart their right to unlimited happiness. It was as if half the young people in America had decided not to grow up. Why should they? Look at the world they were being groomed to serve. What with the Cold War justifying the stockpiling of more and more nuclear weapons and the possibility endlessly canvassed by the media that, after a third world war, there might not be a world to grow up in, the young of the 60s who didn't escape hysterically into drugs or sex, organised to protest. Huge anti-war marches in Washington and Berkley in 1968 and 1969 were followed in 1970 by a demonstration at Kent State University, where six students were killed by armed police. By 1973, President Nixon and Secretary of State Kissinger had no option but to withdraw American troops from all the Indochinese battlefields, leaving Saigon to fall and Vietnam to be united under the Viet Cong. Loss of the war left United States shamed in the eyes of its Cold War allies, with 58,000 American soldiers killed, many more physically and mentally wounded, and a horrifying statistic of between two and twelve million Vietnamese dead, wounded or left homeless in a destroyed country. And yet the United States' disgrace, followed by the ousting of President Nixon, did not, as the young protesters hoped, make an impact on the US policy of foreign intervention, or on the pace of its lethal weapon technology. The real legacy of the Counter Culture was carried forward in the arts, not least poetry, and not only in America but everywhere in the world where the youth culture of the sixties brought its music, its liberated language and its determination in the words of the song, to 'overcome'. Swinging London was a creation of demonstrating

Washington. Ginsberg and Kerouac's raids were not so much *on* the inarticulate as *through* it, like circus motorists roaring through a huge drum.

And here I would like again to intrude a little on my attempt to give a fair account of my contemporaries and their rival anthologies with some testimony of my own. For about eight months in 1969-70 I was a fellow of what was then known as The Radcliffe Institute for Independent Women (now The Bunting Institute). I was married to a lecturer in Chinese History at Cambridge University in England, then a visiting fellow at Harvard, and we had with us our two small boys of about four and five. I could hardly, therefore, call myself an independent woman, but nevertheless, I found a school that would take the children for long enough each day to give me time to research and begin to write a poem I was already calling *Correspondences*. Its subject was not a matter of choice or inspiration; it was a matter of necessity. At the time I could not have written anything that was not a retrospective history of the New England I had known as a child and had found, returning as an adult, to be as alien as if it had been transformed by an invasion from Mars. In 1970, England was only just catching up with the psycho-political trends that an intoxicating mix of Marx and Freud, augmented by writings by such period gurus as Herbert Marcuse, Alan Watts, Paul Goodman and Timothy Leary had spread widely over the US. At that time the new back-to-Blake philosophy had not registered with me or with my husband. I needed guidance even to know where to look for a guide to this curiously self-motivated, protesting and demonstrating youth culture. By sheer luck, I found it in a cheap paperback picked up, I think, in a drug store: *The Making of a Counter Culture: Reflections on the Technocratic Society and Its Youthful Opposition*, by a social historian, Theodore Roszak. I keep this paperback on my shelves to this day as a reminder. Roszak's thesis was convincingly simple. In his first chapter he identified America's managerial democracy as a 'technocracy', i.e. 'that social form in which an industrial society reaches the peak of its organisational integration'.

It is the ideal men usually have in mind when they speak of modernising, updating, nationalising, planning. Drawing upon such unquestionable imperatives as the demand for efficiency, for social security, for large scale co-ordination of men and resources, for ever higher levels of affluence and ever more impressive manifestations of collective human power, the technocracy works to knit together the anachronistic gaps and fissures of the industrial society... So we arrive at the era of social engineering in which entrepreneurial talent broadens its province to orchestrate the total human context, which surrounds the industrial complex.[10]

In such terms, technocracy is not at all the exclusive province of capitalism; it adheres to any system of organised control, from communist to despotic, in which a nation's health depends on a technological heart to keep the fluids of productive economic growth coursing through its arteries. As a technocracy grows and becomes more dependent on specialist knowledge, most of its citizens cease to understand the complexity of its workings, so they refer managerial matters more and more to trained experts who, in turn, refer them to still more specialised experts who appeal ultimately to the authority of science. Beyond science there is no appeal. So it came about that Roszak, in 1969, though critical of the drug-induced, pseudo-mystical hopes and joys of the drop-out generation, turned his well-informed critique into an all-out attack on what he called 'the myth of objective consciousness', by which he meant rational thinking as opposed to spontaneous emotional response and 'the scientific method' as opposed to visionary receptiveness. As one would expect, the poet to whom Roszak eloquently appealed for justification was William Blake, in whose prophetic poems the power-wielding spirits Nobodaddy and Urizen (your reason) appear as the root causes of human misery.

This is not the place to mount arguments against Roszak's (or Blake's) all-out denunciations of reason and the scientific method, though I might just mention in passing that it is a huge mistake to confuse the satisfactions of science and the joy of achieving even a little proof of knowledge for the exploitive

use of science-based technology for selfish or destructive pur-
poses. The quarrel between science's proofs and imagination's
projections is after all an old one. Out of Democritus's ancient
idea of atoms Epicurus (341-270 BCE) constructed a universe
infinite in space and time in which the earth and sun and moon
along with humans, animals, insects and grains of sand all came
about without a creator or designer. Even in his last illness
Epicurus is said to have achieved serenity from contemplating
just such a uncreated, godless universe. Hundreds of years
later, the Roman Lucretius, revived Democritus's atoms in *De
Rerum Natura*: 'It is knowing the way things are,' he wrote,'
that awakens the deepest wonder and most profound joy.' [11]
The dispute (if there really is one) between qualitative truths
claimed by religion and poetry and quantitative facts proven by
science is inexhaustible and because it rests ultimately on
matters of temperament, ability and taste, it will probably never
be settled.

Nevertheless, among the memorable religious believers and
poets of the Vietnam years who would have read and agreed
with Roszak's denunciation of the futility and wickedness of
applying technological thinking to moral and religious questions
was Denise Levertov. Not only was she one of the few women
poets associated with Black Mountain's revolt against the literary
establishment; she was by any standard an intelligent artist, the
only poet of the period to have poems published both in Donald
Allen's *The New American Poetry* of 1960 and a second edition
of Hall's and Pack's *New Poets of England and America*, which
came out in 1962 – a new selection of young poets which this
time was (a little) more welcoming to women. Not having space
to consider the poetry of more than one of these, I have chosen
Denise Levertov as a poet crucially different from myself, yet a
woman I respect and have learned from over the years. I have
selected poems that I judged to be typical of Levertov'e three
memorable voices. The first is an early descriptive poem called
'The Rainwalkers', written under the influence of Black Mountain
but free of Olson's self-conscious method and unwieldy syntax.
As an illustration of Levertov's gift for sensitive observation, both

of nature and of human nature, it seems to me much closer to the spirit of Christian Saintliness or Zen than the bombastic soul-seeking of the Olsonites or Beats. 'The Rainwalkers', which I found reprinted in *New Poets of England and America: Second Selection*, first appeared in *The Jacob's Ladder*, published by New Directions in New York in 1961. It was one of the poems I remember having heard Denise Levertov read in Ann Arbor in that same year.

The Rainwalkers

An old man whose black face
shines golden-brown as wet pebbles
under the streetlamp, is walking
two mongrel dogs of dis-
proportionate size, in the rain,
in the relaxed early-evening avenue.

The small sleek one wants to stop,
docile to the imploring soul of the trashbasket,
but the young tall curly one
wants to walk on; the glistening sidewalk
entices him to arcane happenings.

Increasing rain. The old bareheaded man
smiles and grumbles to himself.
The lights change: the avenue's
endless nave echoes notes of
liturgical red. He drifts

between his dogs' desires.
The three of them are enveloped –
turning now to go crosstown – in their
sense of each other, of pleasure,
of weather, of corners,
of leisurely tensions between them
and private silence.

It's a New York poem, obviously; a simple story, simply told in the almost prose of unaffected free verse. If it owes any debt to Projective Verse it would be in the irregular arrangement of the final stanzas. An old-fashioned 'closed' poet might want to know why Levertov set up a pattern of six- and five-line stanzas only to break the fifth line of the third after that visually so effective 'nave' of liturgical red notes: 'He drifts // between his dog's desires', presumably to avoid summing up the poem too obviously as it flows naturally to completion in the final stanza. I'm sure Levertov would have had an explanation for this – probably to do with content determining form – though I don't suppose such a reasoned feeling would have satisfied my yearning for order. Still, why fuss? The poem is beautiful and tender without being in the least sentimental, and that's what matters.

My second example, like a good many of Levertov's poems, was written in response to personal and political situations to which, hard headed and soft hearted, she responded politically and personally. Without hesitating to use frankly 'efferent' language, Levertov combined prose notes from a book in progress called *Staying Alive* with snatches of free verse. It was 1969. Levertov was teaching at Berkeley at a time of mass student protests against the Vietnam War.

May 14th, 1969 – Berkeley
Went with some of my students to work in the People's Park. There seemed to be plenty of digging and gardening help, so we decided, as Jeff had his truck available, to shovel up the garbage that had been thrown into the west part of the lot and take it out to the city dump.

> O happiness
> in the sun! Is it
> that simple, then,
> to live?
> – crazy rhythm of
> scooping up barehanded
> (all the shovels already in use)
> careless of filth and broken glass
> – scooping up garbage together
> poets and dreamers studying
> joy together, clearing
> refuse off the neglected, newly recognised

humbly waiting ground, place, locus, of what could be our
New World even now, our revolution, one and one and
one and one together, black children swinging, green
guitars, that energy, that music, no one
                              telling anyone what to do,
                              everyone doing,
            each leaf of
            the new grass near us
            a new testament...

And then, the next day, an entry records:

At 6 a.m. the ominous zooming, war-sound, of helicopters
breaks into our sleep.

To the Park:
ringed with police.
Bulldozers have moved in.
Barely awake, the people –
those who had made for each other
a green place –
began to gather at the corners.

Their tears fall on sidewalk cement.
The fence goes up, twice a man's height.
Everyone knows (yet no one yet
believes it) what all shall know
this day, and the days that follow:
now, the clubs, the gas,
bayonets, bullets. The War
comes home to us...[13]

However factually exact and emotionally appealing (or appal-
ling), this is non-aesthetic, even anti-aesthetic language, poetry
that in Heather McHugh's terms *does* purport to be 'about
about'.[14] All meaning with little art, it does what political poetry
usually intends to do: it arouses our sympathies, engages our
anger and all but accuses us of not being party to a culpable
aestheticism. I confess to disliking poetry that Keats said he
hated for having 'a palpable design on us'. On the other hand,

I know that Levertov's political faith in the reality and possibility of goodness was tangential to the religious faith she inherited from her remarkable Jewish-Anglican father. Her best poetry, like Traherne's and Blake's, is visionary. She was exactly the poet Theodore Roszak believed might deliver the technocratic world from the sins of its fathers into the hands of its enlightened children. And, of course, into those of many women, who during her lifetime and since her death in 1997 have been finding in Denise Levertov's poetry a source of strength and wisdom they could never discover in the compelling anguish of a Sylvia Plath or an Anne Sexton. A poem like 'Living', which I am now going to read to you, led the way to a new strain in poetry that has today, I believe, taken hold of sensitive readers' imaginations of whichever gender, replacing a good deal of what in the era I have just been discussing deteriorated into self-destructive despair charged with personal ambition.

Living

The fire in leaf and grass
so green it seems
each summer the last summer.

The wind blowing, the leaves
shivering in the sun,
each day the last day.

A red salamander
so cold and so
easy to catch, dreamily

moves his delicate feet
and long tail. I hold
my hand open for him to go.

Each minute the last minute.[15]

If 'Living' is interpreted as an end-of-the world utterance, a hymn of farewell under pressure of war and multiplying tech-nocracy to the miracle and beauty of life on earth, the simplicity of its repeated refrain weighs against its despair. The sounds and rhythmic pulse of the lines imply universality, a perception that every summer, every day, every minute could be and always could have been the last. The peril of living has always to be balanced against the wonder of life; neither exists without the other. So this poem for me is an epiphany that can't be pinned down to being 'about' any particular time or place or event but has bearing on every one. As Auden declared so rightly, 'poetry makes nothing happen'; and yet in times of seeming hopelessness, the gentle tone and unhurried duration of its language can summon a spirit of renewal.

What Is Poetry?

Above everything else, poetry is words;
and words, above everything else, are in poetry sounds...[1]
WALLACE STEVENS

I spent a good deal of time in my second lecture looking back at the political and social turbulence of the post war 20th century. As Robert Lowell predicted in 'Waking Early Sunday Morning', in the late years of the 20th century small war did follow on the heels of small war in Indochina, Israel, Yugoslavia and Iraq. The USA persisted in a more and more dangerous arms race with the USSR amid communist witch-hunts in Washington carried on against a background of racial violence and the assassinations of President Kennedy, his brother Robert, and the civil rights leader, Martin Luther King. Meanwhile, South Africa was shaken by the horrors of apartheid, Ireland torn by sectarian war, murder and revenge. Is it any wonder that British and American poets on both sides of the stylistic divide were drawn increasingly into loading their poems with political and personal angst? True, the bard's role as a recorder of battles, heroic deeds and death is as old as war itself. But, as I hardly need say, the poets of the 1960s and 1970s, especially in America, were troubled by psychological factors that never would have disturbed Homer. Personal uncertainty, frustration and the pricking of a thousand post-Romantic anxieties and Freudian afflictions accounted for at least three suicides among the most gifted American poets of their time – Sylvia Plath in 1963, John Berryman in 1972 and Anne Sexton in 1974 – giving rise to an expectation that poets, like canaries carried into a collapsing coal mine, could be counted on to pay with their lives for the sins of the misguided generations that begot them. The suicides of Plath and Sexton (both privileged New Englanders who, spared the European war, suffered from nothing but a peculiarly American mixture of sensitivity, ambition, neuroses, and disappointment in their personal lives) nourished the burgeoning women's liberation movement, inspiring a fervent, highly educated generation of women poets in America and Britain to take up feminist causes and campaign for a tradition of their own. That Elizabeth Bishop, to me an early exemplar, would have nothing to do with either the politicising or gendering of poetry impressed me when I was corresponding with her in Brazil, collecting material for a short study of her work for Twayne's United States Authors series (published in 1966). Without Bishop's example, though, I'm sure I would have reached the same conclusion. That women should be recognised as serious poets is, of course, a point to be fought for; Emily Dickinson, Emily Brontë and Elizabeth Barrett Browning were among far too few precursors. But that women poets should be relegated to a different caste, as it were, uniting to challenge male precedents by rejecting them seemed to be handing the power to choose the major poets of any period straight back to the self-interested and usually masculine managers of literary reputations.

Since I have already published two studies of Bishop's poetry, I won't dwell on her work today, and yet there is always more to say about poems like 'The Moose' and 'Sandpiper'. I can never tire of pointing out how this poet wrote of personal experience, not by analysing or confessing her private miseries but by *looking through* them to the empirical conditions of *geography*. 'The Moose' accurately charts a bus trip the poet took in 1946 from Great Village, Nova Scotia, to Boston, through the New Brunswick woods where a moose did actually loom into the headlights; 'Sandpiper' takes place on a beach where a closely observed bird was dodging the incoming waves. In both poems, one feels the underlying impulse was personal: the poet's memories of her Nova Scotia family rose in her mind as she drowsed on the bus; the unsettled pattern of her own life seemed exemplified in the sandpiper's behaviour. And yet in both, the observer's eye informed the poet's ear. She *saw* the moose looming over the bus through the moonlight; she *watched* the bird running in and out of the surf. And so by being momentarily drawn out into the visible world she forgot her self – or to use a more up-to-date term, forgot her *identity*. The she-moose was in a position to enlighten the she-poet because wild animals do not (as far as we know) suffer the tortures of self-doubt. This is why

> Taking her time,
> she looks the bus over,
> grand, otherworldly.

And why, too, the passengers on the bus experienced a mysterious unity, a shared feeling of being drawn together beyond their individual lives in the presence of this otherworldly, perfectly natural creature.

> Why, why do we feel
> we all feel this sweet
> sensation of joy.

In 'Sandpiper', a similar revelation occurs when the poet sees the beauty of the impersonal sand grains.

> The millions of grains are black, white, tan, and gray.
> mixed with quartz grains, rose and amethyst.

For me, a poem's success when it reveals an emotion through images like this – what T.S. Eliot identified as an 'objective correlative' – is a wonderful and enviable achievement. For surely the Romantic's quarrel between what Blake despised as reason, opposing it to imagination, derives from misunderstanding the nature of seeing. The words that open the first chapter of Darwin's *The Origin of Species* are 'When we look...', words that might well introduce not only Elizabeth Bishop's poems, but also Blake's 'London' and 'The Sick Rose'. For it is surely through observation that the arts and the sciences discover common ground. If we consider that all language signifiers, including the symbols of mathematics and science, relate to the world by metaphor, we have to agree with that infuriating philosopher, Bishop Berkeley, that what we know is no more than what our senses tell our brains and our brains create as "reality". The only 'reality' we *know*, as Wallace Stevens insists again and again in the bizarre parade of his poems, is the world that in fullest sense of the word we agree to *imagine*, i.e. our minds tell us exists. It's at this point I'd like to introduce a poem (not by Stevens) that gives us an 'objective correlative', a language picture that a reasoning imagination *can see* and *grasp* immediately – another example of the difference between an 'efferent' and an aesthetic approach to seeing that begs no help from abstract theory. The poem is called 'Weed Species', and it's by the Scottish poet, G.F. Dutton.

These are the trees
that grow straight, seed
of knowledge, planted, fed,
tended line by line to be

felled in a gale
of sawdust and petrol. Not those
over the fence, sown free,
broken by season, strays

swarming with eyes and evasion
pests and diseases, the wry
birch and aspen. Beautiful
weed species.

If we were to discuss this poem's "meaning", we might agree that it equates a plantation of forestry pines with cognitive knowledge, the purposeful language of fact and information, and a natural growth of birch and aspens 'over the fence' with imagination – perhaps the kind of imagination Chekhov had, an appreciation of the randomness of chance or luck that gets us through life, however it turns out. Phrases like 'seed / of knowledge' in the first stanza and 'eyes and evasion' in the third give the simile away but don't spoil the picture. Notice that the poem has something positive to say for both sides of the fence. The pines in their doomed, cultivated rows are indispensable to the making of civilisation and money; the birches and aspens, in luck or out, are 'beautiful weed species' that, like poetry, make nothing (but themselves) happen.

I met the scientist-poet Geoffrey Dutton soon after I took up the post of writer in residence at the University of Dundee in the autumn of 1973. He appeared in my office one morning, a wiry middle-aged man in a suit of shabby tweed that, as he approached, gave off a faint, rather pleasant odour of highland peat. Extending his hand, he mumbled, 'Geoffrey' – as if I should know who Geoffrey was – and produced from a briefcase a manuscript of, I suppose, about a hundred poems. Would I read them and tell him what I thought? My first thought, that he was probably the building's caretaker, was succeeded by surprise when he explained that, while in Dundee he made his living as microbiologist, when not in the lab, he lived with his family in a wild corner of the Scottish East Highlands, where he had created a famous garden (hadn't I heard of it?) against every disadvantage of climate and soil. I took home his poems, most of them short, only three or four stanzas, and read them that evening. I certainly had never seen poems like them. It pleased me that they were not literary; no poet-predecessor that I could see, had influenced G.F. Dutton – not even Robert Frost or Wallace Stevens with whom the not over-modest Dutton claimed affinities. It did not please me quite so much that he avoided upper-case letters in the manner of some avant-garde Americans, although I came to appreciate that his austere style, with its somewhat jingling rhymes, was a personal signature. In any case, I soon persuaded him to join a group of students, townspeople and lecturers I had formed on the model of Philip Hobsbaum's Group in Belfast (to which both Seamus Heaney and Michael Longley owed their early reputations) and later, in Glasgow (where Hobsbaum more or less discovered Tom Leonard, Liz Lochhead and, I suppose, me). I like to think that during those Dundee years, 1973–1975, I helped G.F. Dutton find himself as a poet, as twelve years earlier in Ann Arbor, Donald Hall had helped me. By 1978 Dutton had found an Edinburgh publisher for his first collection, *Camp One*. In 1986, Bloodaxe Books published *Squaring the Waves*, followed by *The Concrete Garden* in 1991, finally bringing out Dutton's Selected Poems, *The Bare Abundance*, in 2002. And yet, and this is what I most liked about him, when he died in 2010, Dutton was still as "unliterary" as when I first knew him. A polymath of many gifts and accomplishments, he not only enjoyed an international reputation as a microbiologist but as a deepwater swimmer had published a book on swimming and as a climber, two volumes of hilarious 'Doctor Stories', written during a ten-year editorship of the Scottish Mountaineering Club *Journal*. I suppose Geoffrey Dutton was known principally as a gardener; his books on marginal gardening became the subjects of radio and television programmes that drew visitors to his Perthshire acres every summer. And yet many among his admirers had never heard of G.F. Dutton the poet. He certainly never cultivated the society of his contemporaries, Norman MacCaig or Edwin Morgan; I had the impression that, being a mite vain of his many abilities, he rather despised them. In any case, Dutton's poetry, though visibly set in Scotland, addresses issues usually regarded as the intellectual property of religion and/or science: mankind's irreversible impact on the earth, for example, or the natural compatibility of science and faith – subjects less multi-gifted, more subjective poets tend to avoid like the plague. Nor does Dutton's local philosophising, any more than Wallace Stevens', always convince. But when it does, his poems are sharp as blades. This one called 'minimal' for example:

it is only the simple sunlight
on a fence post
out of the snow.

and I come to set it upright
at the cost
of a single blow.

then I leave them to the sunlight.
one straight post,
trodden snow.

Again, a verbal picture does the work of a good many theses on the cost to nature of human innovation, for instance, or the price the environment pays for development. And again, the poem's pictorial story reveals layers of meaning that seem clearer for not being explained.

I would like to consider one more of Dutton's poems, this one longer and set as kind of preface to his Selected Poems. The picture here relates to the source of his Highland home's domestic water, so is scientific on one level, personal on another, and a confession of faith on still a third.

The Miraculous Issue

Up from the dark strata
pulsing out through moss
centuries of downpour,
an ever-unfurling spring
alive against the heather,
a bull-nosed sensuous thing
of sunlit question and answer
greening its way downhill
to feed the house clear water.

The faithful on their knees
think it miraculous,
beyond common reason,
in winter warm in summer cool,
quick to bless the season;
when I kneel
wrist deep in its thrust and passion
my fingers feel
that truth of imagination.

Yet a thermometer
there through the year
reads four degrees always;
regardless where truth lies.
I set my measure,
my sweat, my shiver,
beside that halt of quicksilver,
its fix of realities,
its scale before my eyes.

For the water about my hand
answers to life;
and the living imagination
pulses that mercury column
degrees of belief I mark up as truth
to stand by my mind; when little seems true
but to kneel on steep ground
and grasp at a flow
ceaseless and vanishing as faith.[2]

Notice that this poem, roughly yet carefully end-rhymed, is an affirmation of faith, imagination being the source of both spiritual faith and faith in science. The first stanza presents the spring and its issue 'greening its way downhill'; the second introduces 'the (religious and secular) faithful' including the poet, who kneels 'wrist deep' by the stream to acknowledge that its temperature feels warm in winter, cool in summer. The third stanza, with its introductory 'Yet' acknowledges that a thermometer placed there reads the same four degrees, summer and winter, 'regardless where truth lies.' 'Truth' here is the key concept, fixing reality neither on the mercury's measurement nor on the man's measure of his feelings. The miracle affirmed in the final stanza is simply the water itself, which answers both to 'life' and to the poet's 'living imagination'; the two are equivalent, marked up as 'truth'... 'when little seems true / but to kneel on steep ground/ and grasp at a flow' that like faith (and like the flow of life itself) is both ceaseless and vanishing.

A poem like this – rational yet mystical, logical yet paradoxical – looks to have little to do with the arguments for and against poetic tradition I put forward earlier in these lectures. Although always conscious of verbal sounds and rhythms, Dutton paid little attention to poetics and none at all to fashion. 'The Miraculous Issue' is a picture and a statement of belief; it has no political dimension, and its speaker is no more than the expounder of a discovery. Compare it with Seamus Heaney's 'Exposure', from *North*, published in 1975. Heaney is a loveable poet not least because he wanted his readers to share in what for him was discovery and at the same time, self-discovery. It's as if the two were the same thing. The psychic warp on which Heaney weaves 'Exposure' is an open, generous self-consciousness. After invoking home ground in Wicklow (like Dutton's in Perthshire) and an invisible comet that might have been a sign to him, he bursts out, 'If *I* could come on meteorite! (*My italic.*) But no, he is condemned to walk through December's damp leaves, 'Husks, the spent flukes of autumn', imagining the heroic Irish poet he'd like to be, 'His gift like a slingstone / Whirled for the desperate.' The question around which the entire poem revolves is 'How did I end up like this?' By the sixth stanza, this most word-conscious of poets is already 'weighing and weighing' his 'responsible *tristia*', wondering not only what his poetry is for, but lamenting his own inability to meet the demands of a desperate national situation.

> I am neither internee nor informer;
> An inner émigré, grown long-haired
> And thoughtful; a wood-kerne
>
> Escaped from the massacre,
> Taking protective colouring
> From bole and bark, feeling
> Every wind that blows;
>
> Who, blowing up these sparks
> For their meagre heat, have missed
> The once-in-a-lifetime portent,
> The comet's pulsing rose.[3]

Heaney's dedication to poetry, his political conscience and his considerable ambition set the tone for the final decades of the same 20th century that confirmed Robert Lowell's dominance on the other side of the Atlantic. Neither, it seems to me, had quite thrown off the role of 'poet as epic hero' that W.H. Auden ascribes to artists of the Romantic period in a remarkable study, *The Enchafèd Flood*, published in 1951. Here is what Auden had to say towards the end of this extraordinary little book:

The characteristic of the Romantic period is that the artist, the maker himself, becomes the epic hero, the daring thinker, whose deeds he has to record. Between about 1770 and 1914 the great heroic figures are not men of action but individual geniuses... with a religious dedication to furthering knowledge, and the kind of knowledge the artist could obtain was chiefly from himself. Characteristically, the subtitle of Wordsworth's epic poem is 'The Growth of a Poet's Mind'. Faust, Don Juan, Captain Ahab are not really the heroes of their respective books, but the imaginative projection of their creators, i.e., what they do is not really done as a man of action for the sake of the act but in order to know what it feels like to act...The artist who has thus to be at once the subject of his experiment and the recorder enjoys excitement and suffers terrors hardly known before.[4]

The spirit of Romanticism that lingered into what we call the postmodern period was also, of course, an offshoot of "modernism" if we take modernism to refer mainly to stylistic innovations introduced about a hundred years ago by Eliot and Stevens on one side of the aesthetic fence and Ezra Pound followed by William Carlos Williams on the other. What seems to have happened subsequently is that while in the nineteen-seventies and eighties expounders of Literary Theory lorded it over many University English departments, 'making it new' became, among younger poets, almost obligatory – unless they were affiliated with the American Formalists; and they, too, have by now became part of the emerging culture of Poetry for Everyone that has flourished since. Becoming a fan or student of poetry now usually means engaging in a popular creative activity rather than closely studying acknowledged texts. And despite so much having been lost from the poetic tradition, 'now' is, or until recently was, a period I feel myself fortunate to have been part of. In Britain since the war the mufflers have been stripped away from the hierarchies of academic privilege and voices have been heard that might never have summoned self-confidence enough to speak or write in less socially mobile times. Seamus Heaney and Ted Hughes were both working-class boys for whom the great literature of the past was a spur, a revelation. Frances Horovitz discovered her distinctive gift for poetry and drama while growing up in Walthamstow, East London. Frances, whose loss from cancer in 1983 I still feel deeply, was so beautiful a person and so sure poetry was a sacred calling that many of us who knew her in her last years, instead of associating her with the ever-swelling ranks of women poets, thought of her as a kind of secular saint. It was not that she was unworldly or, having been trained as an actress, unwilling to appear before the public. She was proud of her reputation as a reader and did all she could to bring poetry to the ears of everyone she could, from students at the Arvon centres to schoolchildren to thousands of listeners to the BBC. This could be why the *I* of her lyrics, her first person singular speaker, seems so much more than the voice of an individual woman declaring herself. Listen to her poem, 'Rain – Birdoswald', written in the farmhouse she and Roger Garfitt rented near the Roman Wall in Northumberland in the winter of 1981–1982.

> I stand under a leafless tree
> more still, in this mouse-pattering
> thrum of rain
> than cattle shifting in the field.
> It is more dark than light.
> A Chinese painter's brush of deepening grey
> moves in a subtle tide.
>
> The beasts are darker islands now.
> Wet-stained and silvered by the rain
> they suffer night,
> marooned as still as stone or tree.
> We sense each other's quiet.
>
> Almost, death could come
> inevitable, unstrange
> as is this dusk and rain,
> and I should be no more
> myself than raindrops
> glimmering in last light
> on black ash buds
>
> or night beasts in a winter field.[5]

Wallace Stevens, in *The Necessary Angel*, the book in which he expounded his theory of imagination and reality, concluded that poetry was not definable, yet despite being unable to define it, we are never at a loss to *recognise* poetry.[6] Putting aside the amount of verbal and visual propaganda that assaults us today through various branches of the media, how does one 'recognise' that 'Rain – Birdoswald' is that rare phenomenon, a memorable poem, a poem that will last? Consider the words and phrases of which it is made. One immediately responds to the weighted significance of its diction, particularly to the words that so precisely and sensitively evoke the scene they describe: the poet stands under a *leafless* tree in a *mouse-pattering thrum* of rain, the cattle *shift* under an evening sky where *a Chinese painter's brush, moves in a subtle tide*. That the beasts are *darker islands*, *wet-stained* and *silvered* by rain prepares us for those striking verbs, 'they *suffer* night / *marooned* as still as stone or tree'. The quiet shared by cattle, rain, darkening evening and entranced poet, alerts us to expect some sort of revelation, so it should be disturbing to hear at this point that 'almost death could come'. But here death is like a continuum of life, *inevitable*, *unstrange* and not at all frightening. Instead of registering horror or fear, the poet's restrained conclusion dwells on the full reality of time passing, registering acceptance, a yielding up of the self that could be religious – although Horovitz's poem (so like George Herbert's in other ways) makes no reference to belief or 'faith'– as Dutton's 'The Miraculous Issue' does.

Wallace Stevens, in the essay already referred to, proposed that 'Since we have no difficulty in recognising poetry...we may ... say that it is a process of the personality of the poet.' He hastily adds, 'to say that it is a process of the personality of the poet does not mean that it involves the poet as subject' and goes on to distinguish 'the direct egotism' of subjective or what we today would call confessional poetry from 'indirect egotism', which is 'the element', the personal force that keeps poetry a living thing, without which 'there can be no poetry'.[7] In these terms, 'Rain – Birdoswald' is, every time it is read or recited, a living thing, but I should like to offer alternatives to Stevens' terms 'direct' and 'indirect egotism' with regard to the role of its author. The part Frances Horovitz plays in 'Rain – Birdoswald, and I think Geoffrey Dutton plays in the argument of 'The Miraculous Issue', could be termed *centrifugal*; the personal references drive outwards, releasing the ego (both of writer and reader) into a spacious dimension for a moment free of self-consciousness. In contrast, the creative ego of a *centripetal* poem drives inward into a metaphor of psychological entrapment or personal myth that can be powerful – as Sylvia Plath's *Ariel* poems are certainly powerful – and yet binding and even dangerously inescapable. Naturally, this schematic division cannot be regarded as absolute; there are degrees of personal involvement, and the feeling of liberation a poet achieves through having written a poem that abandons centripetal self-expression depends on the poem's effectiveness as art.

If Stevens was at least half right and if in the individualist West poetry can be defined as a process of the personalities of its poets, it follows that there are many poems in which a poet's personality plays no part except as it generates a motivating purpose or transcendent vision. Dante is the poet-seer behind but not the hero of *The Divine Comedy*. That we know very little about Shakespeare's life does not affect our awe when we consider his genius, nor does it prevent successive generations from interpreting and reinterpreting his plays. Stevens himself was a poet who expressed himself by investigating ideas concerning art, reality and imagination that had nothing to do with his personal life or his profession as an insurance executive. A poet I came to know and admire in this tradition (though not in the least like Stevens) was William Martin, whom I met through Frances Horovitz and Roger Garfitt in 1980. Martin had been brought up in Silksworth, near Sunderland, and his poetry grew out of the Methodist faith of the mining community in which he grew up. Before he died in 2010, he had published four remarkable books, *Cracknrigg* and *Hinny Beata* with Michael Farley's Taxus Press in Langley Park before Bloodaxe Books brought out *Marra Familia* in 1993 and *Lammas Alanna* in 2000. The titles are as original as the books themselves. Although

Bill Martin made his living in the audiology department of a Sunderland Hospital, he was moved to write, recite and sing his own versions of hymns and ballads, creating an imaginary world out of the real history, politics and folk-life of Wearmouth and Northumberland, enriching it further with his own art work and with the rhymes and rhythms of street games remembered from his childhood. The Durham Miners' Gala was for him the climactic point of the year, and that drum-thumping, banner-waving occasion, together with the pilgrimage on foot he led every summer from his home in Sunderland to Durham Cathedral, initiated many of his poems. You can perhaps get a general sense of Martin's inimitable gift and mythological imagination from the few stanzas on your hand-out, but above all, Bill Martin's poetry needs to be *heard*. I remember with delight the spontaneity of Bill's readings at the Morden Tower in Newcastle in the 1980s, how at the end of sequence of spoken lyrics he would burst into song, his light tenor voice almost caressing his audience.

1.

The keel took my heart
In full tide it was torn
The keel took my heart
Black blood to his flame

The waggonway fall
Was braked by the river
The horse on its tether
With nose-bag and corn

The keel took my heart
To whistle and wo-lad
Down in his brig of dust
Down to his hot ash breath [...]

4.

The keel played at morning-tide
Bide and abide with me
Keel-brass for my heart blown
Banner-water bidding

Rite blinds were drawn to
Down staithe banks drawn all the way
Hats doffed and held there
In the ebb-tide hush

Down in yon forest
The keel rang my heart away
Black bells of Paradise
Hutton and Harvey change

5.

Foy-boatman blow the flame
Loosen his rope-fast sail
Scorch the wind southerly
Fill it with fire in flood

Blood rages over bar
Out in the molten toss
Fury and friend are lost days
Where you are

The keel sought my heart
In full tide it was torn
It beats every tree on fire
Wagga-pulse fossil dawn.[8]

William Martin's gallimaufry of Christian, Gnostic and
pagan images was that of a visionary on the model of Blake
and David Jones, never of an academic. He was in love with a
dream of Christian saints and scholars in ancient Northumbria,
but his fundamental search (both like and unlike that of Ted
Hughes) was for the Ancient Feminine principle he identified
with the earth itself. This he invoked sometimes in the form of
the Virgin (as in the black Virgin of Montserrat) sometimes in
the guise of a Hindu or Babylonian fertility goddess, but most
often in the explicitly sexual figure of the coal mine itself. It is
not easy to follow the lines of what is clearly a structured plan
of something near worship in each of Martin's illustrated
volumes. A reader needs to listen through the street music for
the shaping sequence of these prayer-like lyrics. If G.F. Dutton's

poems call on reason and science to fortify his homely metaphors of life and faith, William Martin's are grounded in an all out vision of a golden kingdom, the glorious Malkuth or Marradharma his imagination never ceased to celebrate in the culture of labour, poverty and struggle that fed the precious stream of human life he commemorated. The 'Mothergate' to which he frequently refers is the miners' term for the main roadway into the pit; Martin let it stand for the birth canal of his people. 'Lammas' means harvest, a harvest celebration or feast, and Martin's last book, *Lammas Alanna* translates into 'a convoluted harvest' or 'lonnen'. His autobiographical note at the end will do for a guide to all his work.

> I was born in 1925 in a mining village three miles or so south-west of Sunderland. My mother was a Methodist, and on Sundays I rarely missed going to chapel three times. This included Sunday School. I was brought up on hymns and preaching, and lodge banners and the solidarity they proclaimed. But there was also the separate secret culture of the street. Games like Cockerooso, Jack Shine the Maggi, Mountykitty and Hoist the Banner were a great joy for the children of that time. There was little or no traffic. The gas lamps produced pools of light in the darkness. This was our contact with an oral tradition that enriched our lives.
>
> I left school at 14, in the summer of 1939. After this it was a world of work and war. In 1944 I sailed for India in the troop-ship *Orduna*.[9]

William Martin, Frances Horovitz, G.F. Dutton – these 20th-century poets who are important to me, and who, with the possible exception of Frances, worked quite independently of contemporary literary fashion, shared little in the way of outlook but an undeniable compulsion, a mesmerising vision of something that demanded personal articulation. The social mobility of the time played to their advantage, but now that they are gone, I fear our present obsession with crowning new poets before we have taken the old into account may work towards their disappearance. As the cultural democracy T.S. Eliot hated and F.R. Leavis feared increasingly takes hold, critics can no longer count on common fields of agreement as to what is to be praised and what condemned in new poetry; promotion tends to replace criticism and anticipated sales cannot be prevented from determining which names among the poets find publishers. Meanwhile, for good and evil, a booming cult of self-publication relies more and more on the internet. While it's no doubt a good thing that so many people are finding personal satisfaction in self-expression, it's unfortunately true that the more popular and easy to write new poetry becomes, the more it is in danger of losing semantic energy. Like a torrent in flood, much of its over production can't help but be shallow and temporary. It's not that memorable poetry has ceased to be written or that it lacks publishers or university patronage or financial backing from public bodies such as the Arts Council. On the contrary, it could be argued that since about 1960 poetry in Britain has been basking in the postmodern renaissance of a new Elizabethan age.

As for my opinion, I wish I could convince you that prizes, such as they are today, are misleading goals for poets. I am not saying that winning poems do not sometimes deserve to win; I am saying that to judge a poem as good or bad on the basis of what a former prizewinner or famous name finds easy to approve, without taking into account how it is made and what it sounds like, is bad for poetry. It will not do simply to protest against environmental threats or rage against humanitarian wrongdoings. The best poetry succeeds (as Auden knew) when more is implied than is actually said and when what is said stops you in your tracks and sets you thinking. No wonder good poetry is so hard to write! This is not to say that no one should write poetry who isn't a born poet; that would be like saying no one should take piano lessons who isn't a Mozart. No. What I believe should be curtailed is overpraise for the mediocre. A hundred years ago, Eliot and Pound, working from the model of the avant-garde French – Mallarmé, Valéry, Laforgue – introduced into poetry elements of obscurity and mystery that, thrilling to English intellectuals, became a real barrier between the new poetry and ordinary readers. Today the situation has gone into reverse; many ordinary readers are themselves writing poems – and a very good thing that can be so long as they remain readers, too, and adopt critical and self-critical standards, convinced that writing poetry is an art at least as difficult to master as writing music, or indeed as writing clear, comprehensible prose.

In any case, the condition of poetry 'now' has not been my concern in these lectures. My object has been to look back at five or six decades of poetry 'now' that have become 'then', hoping to connect some of its innovations to the 'then' of the future. If poetry is to continue to be poetry in the future it will find ways to make itself new without abandoning its links with a tradition that – as Eliot taught my generation – has kept itself alive through incorporating new voices. If I had to choose one poet among those recently lost whose work has influenced the best being written today it would be Seamus Heaney. At his best, Heaney has left a legacy of verse that, while being made almost entirely out of personal (centripetal) memories, nevertheless manages to avoid being wholly "about" those memories. Heaney's successes are almost always due to his fine sense of what can and cannot be said of his personal experience in either rhymed or loosely metrical free verse, and this is true even of poems like 'Exposure' and the self-defining poems of *Station Island*. In the poem I am going to leave you with this evening, the poet avoids the first person singular altogether. The absence of an "I" in the poem 'Sunlight' – part of the dedication of *North* to Mary Heaney (I think she was his great aunt) – turns memory outward to focus on its real subject, which is "love". Now "love", because of its overuse everywhere, not only in poetry and pop songs but ubiquitously in advertising, is one of the most difficult words to use in poetry today. Heaney manages it obliquely and with such subtlety that what are really very private feelings become impersonally detailed and vivid, yet almost sacred, like religious feelings freed from religious doctrine. Listen.

Sunlight

There was a sunlit absence.
The helmeted pump in the yard
heated its iron,
water honeyed

in the slung bucket
and the sun stood
like a griddle cooling
against the wall

of each long afternoon.
So, her hands scuffled
over the bakeboard,
the reddening stove

sent its plaque of heat
against her where she stood
in a floury apron
by the window.

Now she dusts the board
with a goose's wing,
now sits, broad-lapped,
with whitened nails

and measling shins:
here is a space
again, the scone rising
to the tick of two clocks.

And here is love
like a tinsmith's scoop
sunk past its gleam
in the meal-bin.[10]

How to Read Poetry

My talk (not lecture) this evening might well be called 'How to Listen to Poetry' because much of it has to do with reading with the ear, reading, even if silently, slowly and out loud in the mind. I will particularly touch on how to read with a mind alerted to poetry's special relationship with rhythm, recalling with approval T.S. Eliot's remark that a poem starts as a rhythm or a wave in the mind before it reaches expression in words. I will also dwell on how to let a poem's ideas and imagery work upon your imagination so that you, the reader, contribute an individual and original element to its effect. I confess that I owe much to Ezra Pound's essay, 'How to Read', published as a revolutionary document in 1928, having brought to mind Pound's attack on 'Literary instruction in our institutions of learning'– or as he once bad temperedly expressed it, 'Institutions for the obstruction of learning' – when I was in a temper myself about the way an easy option in Creative Writing is sometimes offered these days as an alternative to the serious study of literature. I have long taken issue with the practice of trying to teach students to write poetry before they know how to read it. I have no objection at all to teaching what you might call Creative Reading. Curiously, the situation now is practically the reverse of that which appertained in Pound's day; instead of being taught by dry-as-dust lecturers to swallow the rules of metre and rhyme like school dinners, students today can be encouraged to be creative and write poems without, so to speak, being nourished by any dinner at all!

Now, please don't imagine I am directing this criticism at the University of Durham; I am well aware that students of

English Literature here are introduced to a whole gamut of literary masterpieces, from *Beowulf* through to the present, without being subjected either to the uninspired pedantry of the late 19th century or (as I profoundly hope) to the theory-laden jargon of the later 20th. After all, I have spent most of my working life in an ancillary position at one university or another, supposedly teaching people to write poems, but in reality trying to impart to them something of the English poetic tradition and craft. Early on in my career – or rather, non-career – as a poet-teacher I discovered that many more people wanted to "express themselves" in poetry and share their life experiences with sympathetic others than cared about the art of poem making. My argument for learning to read poetry tonight rests on the differences between self-expression, therapeutic creativity and social opportunity on one side, and art, which, with its sacred or moral component and indefinable satisfactions never wholly belongs to any one artist or teacher or place or period but to a complex of participators over time.

In former times, individuals habitually found consolation and companionship in literature, much as they did in religion. I think, for instance, of my gentle unquestioning American grand-mother who, without being in the least scholarly or academic, knew many passages of Shakespeare, Dickens, Scott, Emerson and the King James Bible by heart, simply from hearing them read and reading them aloud to her family. Before the radio, before television and long before the invention of the computer, entertainment and education, outside of school, had to be home-made. Poetry, like the Bible, came in precious leather-bound books, with gilded pages and beautifully tooled lettering. I think of Elizabeth Bishop's poem, 'Over 2000 Illustrations and a Complete Concordance', in which the poet recalls her grandparents' family Bible:

> Open the book. (The gilt rubs off the edges
> of the pages and pollinates the fingertips.)
> Open the heavy book. Why couldn't we have seen
> this old Nativity while we were at it?
> – the dark ajar, the rocks breaking with light,

an undisturbed, unbreathing flame,
colorless, sparkless, freely fed on straw,
and, lulled within, a family with pets,
– and looked and looked our infant sight away.[1]

Elizabeth Bishop here laments her inability to sustain the kind of simple belief in the Bible and its engraved illustrations that enabled her grandparents in rural Nova Scotia to escape the ills of modernity. Having eaten of the fruit of knowledge and educated doubt, she looked back nostalgically to the 'infant sight' to which she was forbidden to return in the Garden of Eden.

As the world shrinks and computer technology enables us to communicate instantly with people anywhere on the planet, such anxieties have become universal. The more sophisticated our techniques of verbal and visual communication, the less easy it seems to adapt to human limitations. It seems to me sometimes that the nature of feeling, the actual stuff of human understanding, is changing under the pressure of technology. Instead of being protected by the limits of our small round lives, we can't help being constantly thrown out into a world that is real only to two of our senses: to our eyes and ears. Every day, on one screen or another, we are subjected to pictures of happenings in Syria or Egypt or Afghanistan, or maybe even in London or Newcastle, but we respond only with the engines in ourselves that look and hear. However much we enjoy and learn from films (and there is no question that film-making is the most influential art to have emerged in the past hundred years) we can't help being subject to their persuasions. Hearing without actively partaking in an audial event is not listening; it is being exposed to pre-selected sounds; just as looking *at* is not seeing, in the sense of understanding but exposing our eyes to a selection of images. Through our ears and eyes, then, our passive imaginations are swept into global situations with which we personally have nothing to do except as we feel curiosity or pity or a kind of impotent concern. The point is that we do not feel in ourselves; we suffer or triumph vicariously. And curiously enough, while vicarious feelings can distract us and fill our time and even convince us we are deeply concerned, they have worrying repercussions. After we've spent many hours facing the screen, with our minds receiving messages from two "flat" senses and the rest of us stored away somewhere in the unconscious, when we shut off the screen's social world, say of YouTube or Twitter, and turn back to the real one, it is easy to pretend it's not real. And if we try to explain this world in the self-serving chat and glamorously coloured images of the media, we soon find ourselves in trouble. 'Something must be wrong with me; I'm not happy; I'm not successful. Despite the thousands of new friends I've made through Facebook, I feel dubious as Woody Allen!'

All sorts of consolations and cures, of course, are on offer for malaises of the psyche. Setting aside the still effective but no longer universally believed consolations of religion, society has never been so ready to offer scientifically authenticated cures for individual *angst*. Psychoanalysis and psychotherapies of various kinds, each with its own specialist language, are everywhere available. The National Health Service supplies counsellors and carers professionally qualified to ease suffering after every public crisis or private misfortune. Educational bodies are increasingly geared to combat differences of wealth and class with socially equalising ideas, one of which is (and here I return to my main theme) providing workshops in the creative arts for the purpose of therapy. I think I can even risk saying that, in the public mind, creativity is a word that now has health implications. And, indeed, why not? One of the uses of poetry has always been therapeutic. Think of John Stuart Mill, after his breakdown, discovering Wordsworth, or of Darwin reading *Paradise Lost* on the *Beagle*; or of the young, under-schooled Abraham Lincoln, who never set out to work in the fields for his father without a book in his pocket. As Doris Goodwin writes in her marvellous biography, 'Though [Lincoln] acquired only a handful of volumes, they were seminal works in the English Language. Reading the Bible and Shakespeare over and over implanted rhythms and poetry that would come to fruition in those works of his maturity that made Abraham Lincoln our only poet-president.'[2]

In a wholly different context, we read of George Mallory in 1924, shortly before he fell to his death, sheltering with three fellow climbers in desperate conditions high up on the approach to Everest, pulling from his pack his well-worn copy of a popular poetry anthology, *The Spirit of Man*. 'I began reading one thing or another,' he wrote to his wife. 'We all agreed that "Kubla Khan" was a good sort of poem. Irvine was rather poetry shy, but seemed impressed by the Epitaph to Gray's "Elegy". Odell was much inclined to be interested and liked the last lines of *Prometheus Unbound*. Somervell, who knows quite a lot of English literature, had never read a poem of Emily Brontë's and was happily introduced.'[3]

Mallory's therapy on Everest was hardly 'creative writing'; it was poetry reading of a kind that had given soldiers at the front during the Great War a few moments of relief before almost certain death in the trenches. Poetry resorted to in extreme situations is something like poetry read at funerals and weddings; it has always taken pride of place when an occasion has to be noted down in words for remembrance. A more ordinary setting for poetry was in the home, or at school.

I was fortunate in being brought up in a family of readers-aloud. From babyhood my sisters and I were lulled to sleep with cradle songs and dandled awake to the rhythms of nursery rhymes. My grandmother and mother mainly read us stories. But it was my father who read us poetry, and it is to his reading of Scott's *Marmion* and *The Lady of the Lake*, Browning's 'My Last Duchess' and Matthew Arnold's *Sohrab and Rustum* that I'm sure I owe my ear for the music and rhythms of English verse.

Like the romantic musician he was, my father read the iambic lines of the Victorians and later of Yeats and, of course, Shakespeare, as dramatically as any actor, but he was by no means my only aural inspirer. In the 1940s, school children in the United States were made to learn poems by heart for recitation in class. My sixth-grade English teacher at a fairly rough school in New Haven, Connecticut, was an Irish woman – portly, white-haired, red-faced with what was reputed to be 'strong drink' – but with a fanatical taste for poetry. Once a week we sixth graders competed for a gold star for reciting, and for the first time in that school, I was more often than not a winner. I can still remember lines from Macaulay's 'Horatius at the Bridge', which I used to be able to recite in full.

Then up spoke brave Horatius, the captain of the gate.
'To every man upon this earth, death commeth soon or late,
And how can man die better than when facing fearful odds
For the ashes of his fathers and the temples of his gods.'

Stirring stuff. But for a more notable reason I remember some lines from Longfellow's 'A Psalm of Life'.

Tell me not in mournful numbers,
Life is but an empty dream!
For the soul is dead that slumbers,
And things are not what they seem.

Life is real, life is earnest!
And the grave is not its goal;
Dust thou art, to dust returneth,
Was not spoken of the soul.

I associate one of the memorable experiences of my school days with those lines. For once I had learned the poem by heart, something bothered me about the first verse.

For the soul is dead that slumbers,
And things are not what they seem.

Even aged ten, I could tell that something was wrong here. Sense told me to read the line: And THINGS are NOT what they SEEM, while the metre told me to read it: AND things ARE not WHAT they SEEM. (Four stresses, in trochaic metre, like the rest of the poem.) Having deliberated, I decided that Longfellow must have made a mistake. Luckily, being well versed in Gilbert and Sullivan, I knew how to fix it. One of Little Buttercup's songs from *H.M.S. Pinafore* gets the line metrically perfect:

79

Things are seldom what they seem,
Skim milk masquerades as cream;
High low pass as paten leathers,
Jackdaws strut in peacock's feathers...

So I substituted Gilbert's line for Longfellow's:

Tell me not in mournful numbers,
Life is but an empty dream!
For the soul is dead that slumbers.
Things are seldom what they seem.

I don't remember how Miss Turbot received my metrical correction, but when I recited it to my parents later, they collapsed with laughter. What I had diagnosed as wrong about Longfellow's line was a hitch in the flow of the metre. At the age of ten I hadn't given thought to that most important matter, *the difference between metre and rhythm*. Metre, in English poetry, consists of rules for counting syllables and arranging them in regular beats, like feet walking or clocks ticking. The correct metre for English verse from the time of Chaucer through to and beyond the Victorians was to give an even number of syllables in each line an iambic footfall, i AM, i AM, i AM, that could be reversed as trochees, YOU are, YOU are, or extended by a quick, light anapaestic I am RIGHT, or a dactyl, YOU are right, or even on occasion broken into strong equal beats, SHUT UP, in a vigorous spondee. It was also possible to let an empty beat or pause represent a syllable, usually at the end of a line. (Row, row, row your boat/ Gently down the stream *rest* / is a four-beat couplet.)

Any poet with an ear that instinctively plays with such metrical rules, listens through it, as it were, to the natural rhythms of English speech or counterpoints one against the other, metre against rhythm. It is to this counterpoint in traditional poetry that every poetry reader ought also to listen. Here, for example, are the first five lines of Keats's *Endymion*, which in my old college textbook (to which I still return when at a loss for literary terms) are carefully scanned with a clutter of xes and diagonal strokes. Yet a sensitive reader need not mess with diacritical marks; the poem stands beautifully without scaffolding if in your mind, as Robert Frost recommended, you cross sound with sense.

A thing of beauty is a joy forever:
Its loveliness increases; it will never
Pass into nothingness: but still will keep
A bower quiet for us; and a sleep
Full of sweet dreams, and health, and quiet breathing.

To be sure, a good deal of stopping mid-line and following around of enjambments is called for to make unforced sense of these lines. You can count on your fingers ten or eleven syllables (or five stresses) in each one, but all you really need do is pay attention to the punctuation and read the lines naturally to bring out their interwoven meaning, rhythm and feeling. For a second opinion about the value of dwelling in the feelings of a poem through listening to its cadences as to a living voice, let me call to witness your own David Fuller, whose lovingly perceptive study of Shakespeare's Sonnets (titled *The Life in the Sonnets*) confirms at every level my own conviction that poetry's place in people's lives 'is not dependent on the poetry's subject or its forms' (i.e. metre) but on the *feelings* it conveys through rhythms and words.[4] Far too much is made today, judging from poetry prizes and recent publications, of what poems say, without much regarding their musical or rhythmic components. Ezra Pound's three elements of poetry, though he gives them portentous Greek labels, still apply:

Melopoeia, wherein the words are charged, over and above their plain meaning, with some musical property, which directs the bearing and trend of that meaning.

Phanopoeia, which is a casting of images upon the visual imagination.

Logopoeia, 'the dance of the intellect among words', that is to say, it employs words not only for their direct meaning, but takes count in a special way of habits of usage, of the context we expect to find with the word [...] and of ironical play. It holds the aesthetic content which is peculiarly the domain of [words], and cannot possibly be contained in plastic or in music.[5]

Logopoeia, or word play, is not lacking in today's experimental poetry. Nor is *phanopaeia* or original imagery neglected. *Melopoeia*, however, or the music and inherited rhythm of English poetry, has suffered a sort of blitzkrieg from the ubiquity of free verse and its unrestricted permissiveness. And with the shunting aside of traditionally cadenced lines as vital bearers of feeling, poetry has become much cruder and closer to prose, energised by everyday talk and street-slang – the language of soap operas and police dramas. To my old, bound-to-be-disapproving eyes, it looks as if our youth culture, happy with its gunge-level clothes, punk music and junk food, has been pleased to spawn a kind of throwaway poetry that everyone is encouraged to enjoy (as at a poetry slam) but no one much cares to remember. It's as if bad old imperialist civilisation has been turned upside down and the 19th-century assumption that romantic love, heroic deeds and noble thoughts were the stuff of poetry has been replaced, not by the learned sophistications of the modernists, but by a postmodern appetite for sensational life stories, eccentric language games and a policy of uninhibited self-expression. Eliot and Pound would have been horrified.

Well, complaining is an old person's privilege; and I do often bring to mind that shifts in cultural taste are healthy for the arts; that 'new styles of architecture', in whatever art, usually mean that old ones are played out. Or played out, at least, until their weaknesses have been purged by fresh ideas. We should remind ourselves, too, that for many thousands of years no words were committed to writing at all; there wasn't such a thing. The bard or professional minstrel sang or recited narratives to an audience that knew a common stock of epics by heart. We can even speculate that once writing had become a technologically superior way of preserving myths and heroic stories, as much may have been lost from communal memory, as perhaps was gained in the way of books and libraries.

Peter Redgrove has left us a delightful poem on something like this theme, called 'Song', which reflects on the way the natural joy of religious ecstasy – and by extension, poetic ecstasy – exposes itself to sterility and codification once it is written down.

Song

I chuck my Bible in the parlour fire.
The snake that lives behind the bars there
Sucks at the black book and sweats light;

As they burn together, the codex
Flips its pages over as if reading itself aloud
Memorising its own contents as it ascends curtseying

Like crowds of grey skirts in the chimney-lift,
In particles of soot like liberated print.
The vacant text glows white on pages that are black.

[...]
                              Around us in the parlour
The inn-sign creaks like rowlocks.
The drinkers glower as my book burns.

Their brows look black
Like open books that turning thoughts consume.
Then all at once

With a gesture identical and simultaneous
Of reaching through the coat right into the heart
They all bring out their breast-pocket bibles

Like leather coals and pile them in the fire
And as they burn the men begin to sing
With voices sharp and warm as hearth-flames.

The black pads turn their gilded edges and
The winged stories of the angels rise
And all that remains is our gathering's will

Which assembles into song. Each man sings
Something that he has overheard, or learnt,
Some sing in tongues I do not understand,

But one man does not sing. I notice him
As my song takes me with the others. He is
Setting down the words in rapid shorthand

In a small fat pocketbook with gilded edges.[6]

Redgrove's 'Song' is a fine example of the pleasure to be found in free verse, when a poem does not strain for metrical correctness but yields itself wholly to its rhythm. The rhythm is right for a poem when it delivers both meaning and feeling without calling attention to itself and without deferring to outside pressures. Free verse is the dominant form of contemporary poetry, yet I think it's more difficult for a reader to assess (and for a poet to write) than poetry that conforms to metrical rules. The chief element in free verse is indeed what it says, but it's not that simple. For while on the surface 'Song' appears to be a rather startling little parable concerning the joyous (but short-lived) freedom that might be released by disposing of the Bible and returning to unregulated joys of worship, if you read imaginatively behind that message, you can see that, by extension, it relates to a profound question concerning the nature of human societies. The question 'Song' subliminally asks is: do words, inspirational in the mind and mouth before they are written down, come closer to a full experience of our natures than words fixed immutably in a text? We can extend the question and ask, how much should a society rely on the will of individuals to establish a free but possibly anarchic way of life, how much should it order itself through written words – statutes of law or a national constitution – or the Old and New Testaments. For once a book is written and accepted as sacred or inviolable, it too easily becomes an instrument of absolute power, indispensible in the hands of a virtuous leader, but inhumane and destructive in those of a tyrant. Redgove's poem, to me then, brings to mind still relevant social and philosophical problems that Plato and the Greeks endlessly debated and upon which Shakespeare, in his plays, constantly played variations.

And so the contrary impulses of religion and song still seem, as at their roots, to be inextricably tangled. When inspiration is caught and captured in texts declared to be infallible, art, like faith, begins to run the danger, as in Shakespeare's sonnet, of being 'made tongue-tied by authority'. The temptation of free will to overthrow authority is both dangerous and irresistible. It is this familiar mind-forged tug-of-war that Redgrove pinpoints – lightly rather than solemnly. I myself believe this perpetually active antagonism is a good thing for poetry; it's a sort of metaphysical engine that keeps it from stagnating. We all think we know what we mean when we say we are true to ourselves. We also know what it means to be true to our beliefs. And both "truths" – if you can call attitudes of mind "truths" – have to do with what we most value in our lives.

This is why it's important that we who care about poetry identify it as an art, not primarily as therapy or a vehicle of thrilling sensations or a convenient channel for the exchange of gossip – although poetry can encompass all those things if it is genuine. How do you tell if it is genuine? This is what Marianne Moore had to say in her poem, 'Poetry'.

> [...] when dragged into prominence by half poets the
>   result is not poetry,
> nor, till the poets among us can be
>   'literalists of
>   the imagination' – above
>   insolence and triviality and can present
>
> for inspection, imaginary gardens with real toads in them, shall
>   we have
>   it. In the meantime, if you demand on the one hand,
>   the raw material of poetry in
>   all its rawness and
>   that which is on the other hand
>   genuine, then you are interested in poetry.[7]

The style or period of a poem, in other words, doesn't matter. Its rhythm does. Its diction does. And so does its imagery. All of these intermingle in varying degrees, according to how a poem "gets to" its reader. And that means the reader himself (herself) has to put something imaginative into the poem. As poetry moves away from the past, with its pre-set forms, and closer to the present, reading a poem makes more, not fewer, demands on you. Suppose you open a book of poems and run into a line, 'My Life had stood – a Loaded Gun'. Although you can see that the poem is written in stanzas, you stagger back with amazement – not because it scans in iambic tetrameter, and not because there is a satisfying alliterative link between the words 'life' and 'loaded', and not because it is impossible for a gun to have life except in art, but because all these elements together set your mind thinking and your memory working back to a time, or times, when you, yourself, felt that something was about to go off like a gun in your life. As you read it, you discover that the metaphor that runs through this poem (by Emily Dickinson) stands simultaneously for a gun waiting for its owner to fire it and a woman waiting for the crises that will catapult her into physical love. The poem never makes this claim of course. After the first line, it become clear that the poem is spoken throughout by the gun, veering away from its human tenor and becoming almost surreal as it depicts how a gun in the hands of its master (like a woman in the arms of her lover) would feel:

> To foe of His – I'm deadly foe –
> None stir the second time –
> On whom I lay a Yellow Eye –
> Or an emphatic thumb –

In the final stanza, the gun acknowledges its mechanical nature, its inability to die and achieve immortality, like its mortal master. And this suggests yet another layer of meaning. For we see that the poem has a shadowy Christian dimension.

> Though I than He – may longer live
> He longer must – than I –
> For I have but the power to kill,
> Without – the power to die – [8]

The oddness of this poem, the impossibility of translating it into prose, deepens its mystery and yet detracts not at all from its effect. But to understand this, you have to stretch its meaning far beyond its metred words.

On the other hand, conventional rhymes and metres have not lost ground even today, though with the ubiquity of free verse, readers are apt not to notice whether a poet 'makes mistakes' or not in attempting to write what my fellow Americans call "formalist verse". Since I am running out of time, I won't inflict what I take to be examples of "bad" formal or free verse on you. Instead, here is a little poem by Robert Frost that skirts every kind of contemporary danger by adhering to iambic pentameter couplets while finding in a natural speech rhythm the right images and the right tone and feeling for what it both says and makes us feel.

Moon Compasses

I stole forth dimly in the dripping pause
Between two downpours to see what there was.
And a masked moon had spread down compass rays
To a cone mountain in the midnight haze,
As if the final estimate were hers;
And as it measured in her callipers,
The mountain stood exalted in its place.
As love will take between the hands a face...[9]

It's that final, perfectly metrical line, 'So love will take between the hands a face' that transforms a description of a natural phenomenon into an astonishing picture of human love. Frost's handling of the rhyme and metre is so effortless and at the same time so skilful that a reader scarcely realises that without just those words placed in just those rhythmic relationships, the poem would fail. However, there is one hitch, and let me call it to your attention to it as a final suggestion about how to read 'creatively'. The hitch occurs in the second line,

Between two downpours to see what there was.

Although I count ten syllables in this line, I can't for the life of me count five stresses. It reads like prose:

BetWEEN two DOWNpours to SEE what there WAS.

If I were ten years old, I might be tempted to 'correct it', as I once corrected Longfellow. Today, I either give a stress to 'two' or simply lengthen the time I give to the space between 'downpours' and 'to see', giving the effect of a stress or a pause without actually doing so. I think a sensitive reading does this, giving Frost the benefit of the doubt by breaking, at his behest, with the clock-like metre and letting the speech rhythm show through.

What makes a poem memorable? Ultimately, its power to captivate and hold the mind is mysterious, although Pound's three elements – melopoeia, phanopoeia, logopoeia – get us somewhere in the range of saying why. And yet, of the hundreds and thousands of poems that have found places in what we might call the library of the ages, only a few "stick" in people's memory or get under their skin. Consider A.E. Housman's eight-line lyric (number XL in *A Shropshire Lad*), known to my husband and myself simply as 'Blue Remembered Hills'. Housman was a minor poet who tended to go on to the point of tedium on the subject of doomed youth and the melancholia of passing time. If submitted for a poetry prize in a competition today, 'Blue Remembered Hills' would probably be consigned to the slush pile. A hundred years ago, it might have won first prize. Who cares? What matters to us is that it comes to mind every time we view remembered landmarks on our drive to our cottage in North Wales. All these landmarks are associated with personal memories – of childhood, of the dead, of times past never to be regained.

> Into my heart an air that kills
>   From yon far country blows:
> What are those blue remembered hills,
>   What spires, what farms are those?
>
> That is the land of lost content,
>   I see it shining plain,
> The happy highways where I went
>   And cannot come again.[10]

So poetry may be 'after all personal' – again to borrow a line from Marianne Moore. If so, though I would never discourage anyone from taking it up as a subject for academic study, I believe its true and ultimate lodging is in people's hearts. Prose does much better as a vehicle for explanation, instruction and argument – indeed, for almost everything we need to know. But just as poetry owes its origin physically to the rhythms of our hearts and pacing feet, so emotionally it will endure only so long as we listen to it breathing, telling us, like music, what we don't "know" but only feel to be right when certain mysterious combinations of words, images and, above all, rhythms alert us to our own hidden feelings.

Affinities: Robert Frost and Elizabeth Bishop

I have chosen the title *Affinities* for this talk because the word influences seems to me, if not wrong, not quite right either when we examine how poets interrelate and learn from each other. *Influences* is suspect because it simplifies what happens by setting up lines of succession or categories that make teaching English Literature possible as an academic subject, though literature as taught in schools and universities – a fine, pleasurable field of study in itself – has little to do with the way one writer's work affects another's. That is a mysterious, highly charged and often competitive business, and it relates as much to psychology and individual lives and temperaments as to language and the cultural climate in which such affinities are recognised and seized upon.

Let me give you a personal example. I was "taught" the poems of Robert Frost (well taught) as a high school student in Ann Arbor, Michigan. I liked them all – lyrical meditations like 'Birches' and 'Mending Wall' and dramatic dialogues like 'The Death of the Hired Man' and 'Home Burial' – though Frost was part of the curriculum, so I studied them with a view to the examination at the end of term. Then, it must have been in November 1948, my piano teacher, a university student I adored, arranged for me to give a recital in my parents' living room – the one and only piano recital I have ever given in my life. I don't think I performed terribly well; I was very nervous. But afterwards everybody clapped and ate cake and drank hot, spiced American cider, and I felt pleased with myself. Towards the end of the evening my teacher presented me with a gift, a book, the first page of which bore an inscription wishing me 'many further achievements in music'. The book was *The Collected*

Poems of Robert Frost, and I have carried it around with me as a kind of talisman ever since.

Over the years, of course, my feelings of affinity with Frost and his poems changed as I changed. At 16, I began to write Frost-like poems myself. When I went on to the university I fell under the spell of T.S. Eliot, and presented myself as a thoroughgoing modernist. Released at last into the "real" world, I fled to England – not a poet after all but a distinctly inexperienced teacher at a girls' school in Kent before becoming an English wife and mother. For about seven years, then, I let Frost's poems sleep in a back pocket of my mind, together with my modernist pretentions and, more importantly, an itch in my mind that told me I'd never be happy unless I was writing poetry. It wasn't until I returned to Michigan in 1960 that I, as it were, recovered Frost in the aftermath of discovering the poems of Elizabeth Bishop. It's for this reason that I think of them both as my "family", though as poets, I suppose, they have as much out of common as they do *in*. Robert Frost, born in 1874, was a year younger than my grandmother; Elizabeth Bishop, born in 1911, was three years younger than my mother. As is the way with families, I grew up as a poet under the influence of both, but not without determination to break free and set up on my own.

Now obviously I can't in an hour consider many of Frost's poems, or even all my favourites by Elizabeth Bishop, who published little, but no duds. I have therefore restricted myself to two aspects of these poets' work. The first is technical and has to do with sounds, rhythms, and the differences and similarities between poetry and prose. The second focuses on their approaches to nature, especially their debts to the natural sciences.

Let's begin with the simpler matter of craft. What attracted me to Frost's poems as a teenager and even more impresses me now is a haunting combination of tone, rhythms and ideas. I don't need to remind you that rational ideas – I mean plain sense and logical presentations – became suspect in avant-garde poetry about the time that Ezra Pound came up with his Imagist dictum, 'No ideas but in things' in a bid to outlaw the practice taken for granted in pre-modernist days of seizing upon a subject for a poem and then sitting down to write about it. Both Frost and Bishop were modernists in so far as they were aware of the mysteries of the unconscious that stimulated and nourished the new poetry, but they were far from wanting to make a fetish of obscurity. Frost, with a good high school background in Latin, revered the metrical structure of English verse, and came up with a principle he called *the sound of sense* when he was finding his feet as poet in England shortly before the 1914 War. 'The sound of sense,' he wrote excitedly to a former pupil in New Hampshire, 'is the abstract vitality of our speech [...] If one is to be a poet he must learn to get cadences by skilfully breaking the sounds of sense with all their irregularity of accent across the regular beat of the metre.'[1]

Sense for Frost lay in the inflections of spoken sentences, i.e., in the meaningful tones of voice we respond to in ordinary discourse before or at the same time that we understand the words. He gave as an example: 'You mean to tell me you can't *read?* / I said *no such thing.* / Well *read* then. / *You're* not my teacher.' Whether or not Frost's principle applies to all or even most poetry, it surely explains how Frost himself came to create convincing everyday speech in his dramatic poems: 'The Death of the Hired Man', 'Home Burial', 'A Servant to Servants', 'Snow', 'The Witch of Coos' and many others.

Some of his most famous pronouncements on how poetry comes into being appear in the preface to that very *Collected Poems* given to me by my piano teacher so long ago. 'A poem,' Frost wrote in his preface, 'The Figure a Poem Makes', 'begins in delight and ends in wisdom. The figure is the same as for love.' With Wordsworth, he held that poetry is 'the spontaneous overflow of powerful feelings', but he pushed the figure further: 'It begins in delight, it inclines to the impulse, it assumes direction with first line laid down, it runs a course of lucky events, and ends in a clarification of life...in a momentary stay against confusion.' Towards the end of this compressed essay – only four pages – Frost insists that 'The sound is the gold in the ore' before throwing off a memorable simile, 'Like a piece of ice on a hot stove the poem must ride on its own melting.'[2]

Well, we can see what he meant, although taken literally a piece of ice is nothing like a poem since ice soon evaporates while a poet hopes his poem will outlast his lifetime. Two points I want to make, though, are, first, that Frost was a critical innovator who, in examining his own practice, discovered that the most interesting poems are those that find their meanings as they go along, revealing to the poet something he didn't know before he began writing. Secondly, that this cooperative process between poet and poem comes about when the poet *listens* to lines as they come to him, unconsciously recollecting other poems while mixing these echoes with the pitch and tone of his own words and rhythms. Meaning or subject matter certainly has a place in poetry, though the poem is a poor one if its meaning can be easily extracted in prose from its weavings of sound and sense. Mind you, as he became older, more famous and pleased to deliver opinions, Frost wrote a great deal of what seems to me no more than whimsical doggerel. For years avant-garde critics dismissed him as a popular rhymer, an opinionated pundit, a cracker-barrel philosopher. It was not until Lionel Trilling, on the occasion of Frost's 85th birthday, declared 'The universe that [Frost] conceives is a terrifying universe' that he was generally recognised as a towering, in many ways conflicted figure, particularly as regards his 'terrifying' view of nature.[3]

Now, before looking at one or two of Frost's poems, I'd like to consider what Elizabeth Bishop, in contrast to Frost, had to say about poetry, about what it is or should be and how it comes to be written. Among the unpublished papers she left when she died in 1979, is a draft talk Bishop sketched out but never delivered called 'Writing Poetry is an Unnatural Act'. Here are the first two paragraphs.

Writing poetry is an unnatural act. It takes great skill to make it seem natural. Most of the poet's energies are really directed towards this goal: to convince himself (perhaps with luck, eventually some readers) that what he's up to and what he's saying is really an inevitable, only natural way of behaving under the circumstances.

Coleridge, in *Biographia Literaria*, in his discussion of Wordsworth [...] says, 'The characteristic fault of our elder poets is the reverse of that which distinguishes too many of our recent versifiers: the one conveying the most fantastic thoughts in the most correct and natural language, the other in the most fantastic language conveying the most trivial thoughts.'[4]

I suppose that Coleridge's dictum could apply to poetry now as in her day, but Bishop chiefly drew examples of fantastic thoughts in natural language from the 17th-century divine, George Herbert. She didn't, as she might have, mention Frost. Her tastes, formed at Vassar College in the 1930s, were restrictively highbrow, favouring baroque and metaphysical models. She would have regarded Frost as old-fashioned, too populist and much too famous. So there is no question of her being influenced by his example. Still, I believe that affinities exist between them, and one of these is that they both made a point of studying natural history, having from their college days, found inspiration in Charles Darwin's *The Voyage of the Beagle*. I also believe that if Frost had read Bishop's poems, he would have approved emphatically of the three qualities she said she admired most in poetry: *Accuracy, Spontaneity and Mystery*. I will be referring to these qualities as touchstones in what follows.

Let's look first at an early poem of Frost's, written as long ago as 1892, when he was 18, called 'Now Close the Windows'. I hope you will be able to hear how the voice-tones naturally strike across the metrical lines – although this, with its Georgian diction, ('ere', for instance) was written long before he came up with his principle of sound and sense.

Now Close the Windows

Now close the windows and hush all the fields: [*dactyl metre.*]
   If the trees must, let them silently toss;
No bird is singing now, and if there is,
                  [*a shift in metre to speech-iambic*]
   Be it my loss.
[*In the 4th line, every word is separated, slowing the rhythm down.*]

It will be long ere the marshes resume,	[*dactyl again*]
It will be long ere the earliest bird:	
So close the windows and not hear the wind,	
But see all wind-stirred.	[*again, a syllabic rubato*]

This is a poem about seeing that relies for its effect on hearing. In both stanzas, the lulling dactyl metre catches the ear before the shortened final line of each stanza slows its running pace down. Frost remained faithful to rhymed stanzas and blank verse all his life, and it's perhaps because of his rhythmic conservatism that the disturbing material in many of his poems is easily overlooked. The conclusion of the famous 'Stopping by Woods on a Snowy Evening', for example, confesses to a desire to sleep that suggests death would not be unwelcome if the poet had no promises to keep. Equally well-known, 'The Road Not Taken' concludes 'I shall be telling this with a sigh / Somewhere ages and ages hence: / Two roads diverged in a wood, and I – / I took the one less travelled by, / And that has made all the difference.' The subject provokes the sigh; the right choice is often the most unprofitable, and no one can be in two places at once. One of the chief attractions of poetry is that, in a few words or a single image, it can say one thing and mean at the same time another, or many others. At his best, Frost was eerily effective in presenting his readers with parables of the human predicament. 'The Road Not Taken' is biblical in its simple presentation of the indivisible nature of choice. Indeed, Frost grew up steeped in the stories and teachings of the Bible, taught by his Swedenborgian mother to regard it as the staple of his spiritual life. Nor did the poet ever abandon his faith in what over the years became an increasingly eccentric take on Christian philosophy. Late in his life he wrote two short morality plays, 'A Masque of Reason', recording a debate in Heaven between Job, Job's Wife and a very personable God, and 'A Masque of Mercy' which opposes the idea of God's Justice to that of New Testament Mercy, setting the ideological drama in a bookshop of human records, with biblical characters ranging from the prophet Jonah, to St Paul to a disillusioned, good-natured woman named Jesse Bel (Jezebel).

Yet despite his Christian bias, Frost had inherited, possibly from his father (a brilliant but feckless newspaper man who died of drink and TB in San Francisco when Robert was 11), a burning curiosity to learn as much as he could about the world he had unwittingly been born into. As Jay Parini, in his fine biography of Frost, remarks,

> Almost uniquely among the modern poets, Frost was interested in science, and he knew a great deal about physics, astronomy, botany and geology [...] In effect, his engagement with science kept him from falling into sentimental attitudes toward religion or the human heart, making it possible for him to write poems such as 'The Most of It' and 'Desert Places'.[5]

It is to these scientifically slanted poems that I want to turn now. Unfortunately, we have time to consider only a few. The two best-known, 'Design' and 'The Most of It', both surely influenced by Darwin, are in no way irreligious. Consider 'Design'.

> I found a dimpled spider, fat and white,
> On a white heal-all, holding up a moth
> Like a white piece of rigid satin cloth –
> Assorted characters of death and blight
> Mixed ready to begin the morning right,
> Like the ingredients of a witches' broth –
> A snow-drop spider, a flower like a froth,
> And dead wings carried like a paper kite.
>
> What had that flower to do with being white,
> The wayside blue and innocent heal-all?
> What brought the kindred spider to that height,
> Then steered the white moth thither in the night?
> What but design of darkness to appall? –
> If design govern in a thing so small.

Applying Elizabeth Bishop's critical criterion, here is descriptive *accuracy* (the flower, the spider and the moth), *spontaneity* in the sonnet's self-discovering language, and most of all, perhaps, *mystery*, manifest in the last two lines that turn the poem around and bring to mind Darwinian evolution questioning the motives of a Designer. What is disturbing, even shocking, is the implication that a Creator who chooses to upset nature with such small irregularities would more likely be malignant than benevolent. A Manichaean conflict between light and dark, good and evil is suggested, but here evil is associated with unholy whiteness, like leprosy or arsenic. So, from one point of view, 'Design' is a spooky poem, the kind of moralised tale of New England witchery that Frost enjoyed, harking back to his New England predecessors, Hawthorn and Melville. On the other hand, that an albino spider should have caught a white moth and found refuge in a white flower could be taken as a proof of natural selection working either in favour of mutation or against it. The chance selection, as a scientist would see it, could have nothing to do with a Creator. Whiteness would have made the spider a conspicuous prey to any bird out to get its breakfast. In another poem paired with 'Design' in the *Collected Poems*, 'On a Bird Singing in Its Sleep', Frost specifically picked up the thread of natural selection.

> It could not have come down to us so far,
> Through the interstices of things ajar
> On the long bead chain of repeated birth,
> To be a bird while we are men on earth,
> If singing out of sleep and dream that way
> Had made it much more easily a prey.

Perhaps the strongest of Frost's tributes to nature's autonomy, demonstrating his understanding of its evolutionary independence – if not of God, certainly of man – is that extraordinary poem called 'The Most of It'.

> He thought he kept the universe alone;
> For all the voice in answer he could wake
> Was but the mocking echo of his own
> From some tree-hidden cliff across the lake.
> Some morning from the boulder-broken beach
> He would cry out on life, that what it wants
> Is not its own love back in copy speech,
> But counter-love, original response.

And nothing ever came of what he cried
Unless it was the embodiment that crashed
In the cliff's talus on the other side,
And then in the far-distant water splashed.
But after a time allowed for it to swim,
Instead of proving human when it neared
And someone else additional to him,
As a great buck it powerfully appeared,
Pushing the crumpled water up ahead,
And landed pouring like a waterfall,
And stumbled through the rocks with horny tread,
And forced the underbrush – and that was all.

Commenting on this poem in the year before he died, Frost called it an 'extravagance' not a 'doctrine', arguing that the speaker, in calling out for something he couldn't have – he couldn't keep the universe alone – missed the *wonder* of what he could have – the magnificence of the buck. The speaker had 'missed it all. All he got was this beautiful thing, didn't he?'[6] And that was enough. The buck was one of the marvels of creation, and the speaker missed it because he couldn't imagine a Creator as anything but someone like himself who would, if called for, overwhelm him with fatherly love. Like Wordsworth, like Thoreau, in some ways like Ted Hughes, Frost thought of himself as belonging to the Western tradition of natural philosophy, holding that the earth was never created for mankind's exclusive benefit. This is why Frost was prepared to be 'terrified' by nature's a-human ruthlessness as he was, or pretended to be, by the spider and the moth in 'Design'.

And yet, while admiring Darwin, Frost never considered himself to be an unbeliever. As for Darwin's own views, two generations before Frost's, we know how unsympathetic they were to any belief in *Homo sapiens*' right to nature's special attentions. In 1838, two years after returning to England on the *Beagle*, Darwin scribbled in his notebook, 'Man in his arrogance thinks himself a great work. worthy the interposition of a deity, more humble & I believe true to consider him created from animals.'[7] Still, it would be a mistake, I think, to accuse Darwin of setting up science to refute religion. He in no way set himself up in opposition to belief. And Frost, who was neither a Transcendentalist nor a scientist nor even a conventionally Romantic poet, probably would have gone along with that in his playful, quizzical way.

Elizabeth Bishop, no less than Frost, was drawn to poetry by the beauty of its sound and form, and like Frost again, she came to it through trying personal circumstances. Her well-to-do father died shortly after her birth in Massachusetts, leaving her to the care of an inconsolable mother who was soon to be confined in an asylum for the rest of her life. Her mother's family, Baptists in rural Nova Scotia, gave the child a warm home and devoted care until, at the age of six or seven, little Elizabeth was snatched away from the grandparents she loved to be educated by her father's family, who sent her to a private boarding school and Vassar College. For many years she was torn between deeply affectionate feelings for her Nova Scotia family and a grudging consciousness of debt to her father's, which she felt had unsympathetically put her in the way of an excellent education and sufficient economic freedom to become a freelance poet and artist. The poems she wrote while at Vassar were strained artificial attempts to write without reference to her disturbed personal life, and it was not until she worked out a way of telling her home truths 'slant' (to borrow Emily Dickinson's phrase) that she developed her unique voice. Her first "real" poems, such as 'The Map' and 'The Imaginary Iceberg' were written when she was a shy, unhappy young woman living alone in New York City. These were not only fine examples of art, they were chiefly *about* art. She produced nothing that had much to do with nature until she found happiness with a college friend in Key West, Florida. Here there was no avoiding her natural surroundings, and perhaps because the south held no memories for her, she found herself free to open her mind to the experience of an exotic 'Florida', its landscape, its people and its creatures.

The first of Bishop's poems to grab my attention was 'The Fish'. I still can feel the thrill of first encountering the poem's vivid descriptive detail, its short breath-like lines and its wonderful build up to an epiphany at the end. The details become more and more pictorial as they accumulate: the fish's skin that hangs in strips 'like ancient wallpaper', its pattern of 'full-blown roses / stained and lost through age'. Can't you just see it? Then those barnacles covered with 'tiny white sea lice', his gills 'breathing in / the terrible oxygen'. And so the poem proceeds until she observes that 'from his lower lip − / if you could call it a lip − / [...] hung five old pieces of fish-line [...] grown firmly in his mouth'.

> A green line, frayed at the end
> where he broke it, two heavier lines,
> and a fine black thread
> still crimped from the strain and snap
> where it broke and he got away.

As details accumulate, the fish becomes an emblem not only of its own survival but of survival itself, a evolutionary triumph of heroic persistence. The most astonishing thing about the fish is that it isn't human. It's this sudden realisation that prompts the fisher-poet to let the fish go.

> I stared and stared
> and victory filled up
> the little rented boat,
> from the pool of bilge
> where oil had spread a rainbow
> round the rusted engine
> to the bailer rusted orange,
> the sun-cracked thwarts,
> the oarlocks on their strings,
> the gunnels − until everything
> was rainbow, rainbow, rainbow!
> And I let the fish go.

The word, 'victory' − the only abstract noun apart from 'wisdom' allowed into the poem − gives notice that all the accumulated details have built up to a change of focus. Delight has led to wisdom and 'a temporary stay against confusion' with the victory, not really of the fish but of the fisher-poet who has overcome a pettiness, like D.H. Lawrence in his great poem, 'The Snake'. And though Bishop, a thoroughly modern artist, avoided philo-sophising about where her poem had taken her, surely the oily rainbow spread in the bilge pool reflects the Biblical rainbow revealed to Noah after the flood. In the language of poetry, the rainbow is a confirmed symbol of peace and unity. At the same time, it is a prismatic breakdown of light that invariably displays the same arrangement of colours; the rainbow is as much the material of the scientist as it is of the poet.

You will by now, I hope, have got the drift of this talk, though I'm having to cut it short of needful examples. Elizabeth Bishop, like Robert Frost, was brought up on the Bible in an atmosphere of unquestioning faith, which remained with her as a poignant memory in her later life. Yet, Darwin captured her imagination as soon as she read him. As a further complication, she was aware that her weird, dream-like imagination also pulled her in the direction of Freud. So at least three layers of consciousness and unconsciousness underlie her poems. The faith of her mother's people lay at the bottom, as is evident in the poem 'Over 2000 Illustrations and a Complete Concordance' (quoted in the talk that precedes this) towards the end of which, frus-trated by the inconclusiveness of her travels abroad, she recalls the illustrated Bulmer family Bible she had pored over as a child, its gilt edges rubbing off the pages 'pollinating' her fingertips – again, a scientific word to describe a spiritual sensation.

The lyric nostalgia here, the longing for the illustration's simple answer to the grown woman's searing questions is con-soling so long as 'infant sight' is looked away and replaced by memory. It is by looking that the adult learns, not by thinking or arguing. There seems to be no question that the grown-up Elizabeth Bishop no longer found religious reassurance in this Nativity scene and yet was left with something more valuable than belief. For how would she have managed as a woman and an artist without that wonderfully enduring ability of hers to recall every detail of her past? It was enough for her to know the world existed in all its variety and mystery, the worst and the best of it. And terrible as it often was for her, looking and writing truthfully about what exactly she saw and felt, she was able to find reassurance in what was for her the slow, frustrating, exhausting work of writing poems. For every poem had to be both visually accurate and aesthetically satisfying, each successful achievement was a step, a painful step maybe, but still a step towards making life bearable.

I have suggested that Bishop's escape to Florida from New York and the surrealistic imagery of city poems such as 'The Man-Moth' and 'The Unbeliever' turned her mind to writing more naturally. In 1951, following in the wake of Darwin's *Beagle*, she took a cabin on a merchant ship bound around the southern tip of South America for Europe. She got no further than Rio di Janeiro, where, after falling ill, she began to share a life with a Brazilian aristocrat, Lota de Macedo Soares. Almost immediately her poetry made a further shift in the direction of geography and natural description. She was living in Brazil in 1962 when the editors of the Twayne United States Authors Series in New York commissioned me to write a short book on her work. Nothing much being available in libraries, I approached Marianne Moore for information. The formidable but kindly Miss Moore provided me with addresses in Rio and Petropolis, and urged me to write to Miss Bishop, which I did. I was lucky that in the course of that correspondence (published by Farrar, Straus and Giroux in 2011) Elizabeth Bishop revealed a great deal about her beliefs and practices as a writer. In a letter of 8 January, 1964, she acknowledged her debt to Darwin.

> I can't believe we are wholly irrational – and I do admire Darwin! But reading Darwin, one admires the beautiful solid case being built up out of his endless heroic observations, almost unconscious or automatic – and then comes a sudden relaxation, a forgetful phrase, one feels the strangeness of his undertaking, sees the lonely young man, his eyes fixed on facts and minute detail, sinking or sliding giddily off into the unknown.

The phrase, 'sliding giddily off into the unknown' may not do justice to Darwin's wonder as he went about his naturalist investigations, but it certainly characterises Elizabeth Bishop's approach to her art. Like Marianne Moore (and Robert Frost) she believed that the poet and scientist work 'analogously' but to different purposes. The scientist accumulates facts continually to test hypotheses; the artist is concerned with sense data only as s/he feels them subjectively to be important. And yet ethical, aesthetic and I would say mystical considerations arise in both disciplines, which after all are confined to the operations of the human brain and are alike bound by human limitations. What lies beyond the limits of our human senses and knowledge – in mathematics as in psychology and the wildest imaginations of the mystic – are absolute mysteries that poems can only hint at but never wholly represent. It is enough, as Randall Jarrell once put it, to stand out in thunderstorms all one's life in hopes of being hit by lightning.

Now, I confess that in my own life I haven't been able to stop standing out in thunderstorms where occasionally, only occasionally, I've been struck by insights that eventually, after many drafts, became poems. I learned from her letters that Elizabeth Bishop also worked from life in this way. Towards the end of her beautiful poem, 'At the Fishhouses', set in Nova Scotia, Bishop slipped into a passage I am sure she hadn't anticipated when she began to write it. She described it herself as a *donnée*.

The water seems suspended
above the rounded gray and blue-gray stones.
I have seen it over and over, the same sea, the same,
slightly, indifferently swinging above the stones,
icily free above the stones,
above the stones and then the world.
If you should dip your hand in,
your wrist would ache immediately,
your bones would begin to ache and your hand would burn
as if the water were a transmutation of fire
that feeds on stones and burns with a dark gray flame.
If you tasted it, it would first taste bitter,
then briny, then surely burn your tongue.

> It is like what we imagine knowledge to be:
> dark, salt, clear, moving, utterly free,
> drawn from the cold hard mouth
> of the world, derived from the rocky breasts
> forever, flowing and drawn, and since
> our knowledge is historical, flowing and flown.

What one feels here is that a break though the limitation of knowledge is about to be achieved just as the poet confirms that knowledge is historical. It is not only knowledge that is 'flowing and *flown*' – a brilliant touch; flown is the past participle of fly, not of flow – but so is time itself, represented by the 'dark, salt, clear, moving' utterly inhuman sea. Fire and ice alike burn and freeze, offering no comfort, only the enticement of a numbed escape from the human sphere altogether. Any pull in the direction of despair however, is annulled instantly by the sheer beauty of Bishop's lines, hypnotic and repetitious like a sung litany, setting her (and us) 'utterly free' – as free as Frost, released by the sight of his swimming buck from the punishment of keeping the universe alone. For me, Frost's best poems give voice to a like epiphany – his great late poem 'Directive', for example – though they don't always press home the marvel of it. More often, as in 'Design', he acknowledges fear or awe, taking refuge in a twinkle of humour, or a human drama or an occasional confession that shies away from the inhuman universe, electing to ignore it – as at the end of his poem, 'Desert Places'.

> They cannot scare me with their empty spaces
> Between stars – on stars where no human race is.
> I have it in me so much nearer home
> To scare myself with my own desert places.

The poem of Bishop's that begs to be set next to Frost's 'The Most of It' is obviously 'The Moose' – possibly her finest poem and one she spent 25 years writing before she judged it ready to expose in print. It takes place in one and then the other of the two landscapes that Elizabeth Bishop made imaginatively her own. The first we may call 'geographical' and opens our eyes to the actual scenery though which the bus passed that carried her overnight on a germinal trip from Great Village, Nova Scotia, to Boston in August 1946 – when presumably she conceived the poem. The other is that country of memory and dream we meet in early poems such as 'Love Lies Sleeping' and 'The Monument'.

Composed of 26 six-line stanzas, with more or less three stresses a line, 'The Moose' is phrased like prose and rhymed so naturally that, reading it aloud, one scarcely notices it is poetry at all – a model, if there ever was one, of how to make the unnatural act of writing a poem seem as natural as breathing. The scenery described is an exact topographical description of the Minas Basin around the Bay of Fundy. We are told about the red soil and the river's wall of brown foam, of the fog settling into beds of sweet peas and cabbages; we say goodbye to the sugar maples, the elms, the clapboard churches and farmhouses. As the bus journeys west, we watch a lone traveller (Bishop?) give kisses and embraces to relatives before boarding the bus. Then, night and dreamtime arrive together 'as we enter / the New Brunswick woods, / hairy, scratchy, splintery; / moonlight and mist […] // The passengers lie back. / Snores. Some long sighs. / A dreamy divagation / begins in the night, a gentle, auditory, slow hallucination […]'

It's just here that the thin border line between daylight's routine journey and the night's dreamy one disappears as other lives from other times are overheard talking at the back of the bus.

Grandparents' voices

uninterruptedly
talking, in Eternity […]

Talking the way they talked
in the old featherbed,
peacefully on and on,
dim lamplight in the hall,
down in the kitchen, the dog
tucked in her shawl […]

> – Suddenly the bus driver
> stops with a jolt,
> turns off his lights.
>
> A moose has come out of
> the impenetrable wood
> and stands there, looms, rather,
> in the middle of the road.
> It approaches; it sniffs at
> the bus's hot hood.

Without warning, disrupting the whispering of these family ghosts, the poem, like the driver, suddenly breaks, jolting poet, passengers and readers into the same shocked awareness of an other-than-human presence like that Frost observed in the great buck in 'The Most of It'. We have been prepared by the grandparents talking in eternity for something otherworldly to happen, and indeed it does happen, the moose appears out of another world, the extraordinary world of nature that refuses to prioritise man, that will not allow him, awesome as are his abilities, to keep the universe alone. The appearance, the apparition of this huge, ungainly, ugly animal is a true revelation, a real epiphany, but far from being supernatural, it is just the reverse; a moose, not an angel, brings tidings of joy.

> Taking her time,
> she looks the bus over,
> grand, otherworldly.
> Why, why do we feel
> (we all feel) this sweet
> sensation of joy?

I could talk for hours about Elizabeth Bishop's achievement in 'The Moose', about how it fulfils her every requirement for poetry – accuracy, spontaneity and mystery – and how at the same time it keeps faith with Frost's principle of the sound of sense, and indeed, always sounds like sense, free of a regular metre while establishing a rhythm that moves the poem on without ever forcing its tone.

My time is running out, but before I stop for questions, I'd like to lead you in the direction of one last poem, Elizabeth Bishop's 'The Sandpiper', which again takes us to Nova Scotia and a self-portrait in a geological, geographical mirror of Bishop herself.

> The roaring alongside he takes for granted,
> and that every so often the world is bound to shake.
> He runs, he runs to the south, finical, awkward,
> in a state of controlled panic, a student of Blake.
>
> […]
> His beak is focused; he is preoccupied,
>
> looking for something, something, something.
> Poor bird, he is obsessed!
> The millions of grains are black, white, tan and gray,
> mixed with quartz grains, rose and amethyst.

Writing on 'The Sandpiper', Seamus Heaney commented, 'No writer is more positive in registering the detailed marvels of the world [than Bishop], yet no writer is more scrupulous in conceding that there are endangering negative conditions which must equally and simultaneously be accounted facts of life.' The poem, 'has about it a touch of comedy and a hint of self-portraiture'. [8]

As a piece of self-portraiture, the line to look out for is 'in a state of controlled panic, a student of Blake', recalling Blake's quatrain in 'Auguries of Innocence':

> To see a World in a Grain of Sand,
> And Heaven in a Wild Flower,
> Hold Infinity in the palm of your hand,
>   And Eternity in an hour.

But what Heaney has not commented on is how different Blake's way of looking was from Elizabeth Bishop's! Blake, the seer and creator of his own world-myth, never doubted the validity of an anthropocentric universe. With a directive from heaven, he indeed thought he kept the universe alone. But Elizabeth Bishop, like her sandpiper, thought nothing of the kind. Heaney picked up her pivotal word 'finical... fussy'. Bishop's bird 'runs, he runs to the south, finical, awkward... looking for something, something, something', and therefore he sees all that is possible for a sandpiper to see. Where Blake saw a world (an imaginary world) in a grain of sand, Bishop saw that no grain of sand is exactly like any other; each has been ground down from rocks millions of years older than any form of human life into a tiny grain with its own characteristic colour. Bishop's vision, in short is that of a scientist-artist, 'no detail too small'. Infinity and Eternity are grand matters, the concern of poets who were less observant than Bishop – and less happy, perhaps, playing, like Isaac Newton, with pebbles on the sand – with 'millions of grains [...] black, white, tan, and grey, / mixed with quartz grains, rose and amethyst'.

Epiphanies Among the Poems of Wallace Stevens

As everyone here no doubt knows, the word epiphany – Greek *epiphaneia*, an appearing – has a religious origin. It means a manifestation or showing forth of a supernatural or divine reality. With an upper case E, it refers specifically to the Christian festival held on January 6th commemorating in the Western Church the manifestation of Christ to the Magi. Used metaphorically and with a small e, the word can be stretched to express that feeling of personal exaltation that is sometimes evoked by a certain kind of poem. There are, of course, many kinds of poem, and who would want to limit their scope or variety? But for some years now I have kept a record, a sort of diary in my mind, of poems I think of as epiphanies, poems that have struck me with the force of revelations. I suppose these poems must be termed influential, since I probably would not have written poems myself without their example, but their influence has not been obvious to me; that is to say, I don't believe I've been tempted to imitate them – or at least not for a long time. Instead, they have given me patterns of sounds and rhythms in words that have stayed with me like echoes.

Naturally, over the years my tastes have changed. On the whole, though, I have returned again and again to the poets I call 'seed poets', ranging from John Donne, George Herbert and the 17th-century divines through to Blake and Yeats and on to the Robert Frost and Elizabeth Bishop, whose poetry I have trumpeted faithfully for many years. What I'd like to do this evening in the fifty or so minutes at my disposal is to read with you several poems by a major 20th-century American, Wallace Stevens. All are among those I revere, though few of them conform to a type that an unquestioning Stevens scholar might consider typical, for I am by no means an admirer of all or even most of Stevens' elaborations. A few famous ones, such as 'The Comedian as the Letter C' and 'The Man with the Blue Guitar', prized and praised for their ornate, aesthetically fanciful language, in parts amuse but eventually exhaust me; while his long, philosophical poems on the nature of reality and imagination (all essentially about how in poetry imagination creates its own reality) once they have been taken to pieces and put together again as rational arguments can be irritating – not least because Stevens often argues in the same poem that rationality has no place in poetry. Yet for all his high-spirited verbosity, self-contradiction and pundit-like generalisations, Stevens was, I believe, a great poet. I also want to suggest that Stevens at his most serious and inspired, can be said to honour, while suitably modifying, T.S. Eliot's historically defined tradition of poetry in the English language.

This is the kind of poetry I found myself describing (or defending) last year in an article for a reference book of contemporary poets:

> A poem succeeds when form and subject matter perfectly coalesce, when form is not sacrificed to meaning or meaning squeezed uncomfortably into pre-set forms. Every poem that lasts is more than its subject; each is a work of art in which the elements of life and language, different though they are, have undergone, like a chemical reaction, a transformation in the poet's mind into something 'rich and strange'.[1]

We are not talking here of what poems *say* but of what poems *are*, of what I take Stevens to have meant by a passage in his essay, 'The Noble Rider and the Sound of Words', which opens the discursive prose of his book *The Necessary Angel*:

> Above everything else, poetry is words; and words, above everything else, are in poetry sounds [...] A poet's words are of things that do not exist without the words.[2]

Also relevant to his theory of the complementary roles reality and imagination play in poetry (reality is bearable only as the poet's imagination transmutes it into art), he launches towards the end of the same essay into a defence – unfashionable in his day as in ours – of the word 'nobility':

> The imagination gives to everything it touches a peculiarity, and it seems to me that the peculiarity of the imagination is nobility [...] I mean the nobility which is our spiritual height and depth [...] For the sensitive poet [...] nothing is more difficult than affirmations of nobility and yet there is nothing that he requires of himself more persistently, since in them [...] are to be found those sanctions that are the reasons for his being and for that occasional ecstasy, or ecstatic freedom of the mind, which is his special privilege.[3]

Since there is probably no word more unacceptable among today's popular poets than the word 'nobility' (unless it is 'élitist') I think we must try to forget that Stevens has been pigeonholed as a modernist and consider that he was an American poet whose temperament, like Walt Whitman's and Emerson's, was in everything but the doctrines of religion, religious. In the absence of belief, Stevens' tireless explorations of western philosophy convinced him that civilisation in the 20th century could no longer seriously credit the existence of God. This is how Stevens explained and justified poetry to his friend, Henry Church, who in 1940 tried and failed to set up a Chair of Poetry for him at Princeton.

> The major poetic idea in the world is and always has been the idea of God. One of the visible movements of the modern imagination is the movement away from the idea of God. The poetry that created the idea of God will either adapt it to our different intelligence, or create a substitute for it, or make it unnecessary [...] The *knowledge* of poetry is a part of philosophy, and a part of science; [but] the *import* of poetry is the import of the spirit. [*My italics*][4]

So Stevens, in his passion to rethink the idea of God and the theory of poetry, came all out for spirituality in his essential poets (the above paragraph is only one instance out of many similar declarations). In and throughout all his writing he summoned words – the more extravagant and imaginative, the better – to replace the idea of God with the idea of a supreme fiction, a verbal creation of the imagination powerful enough to give the effect of a spiritual revelation or epiphany. Such an epiphany, for Stevens, was a revelation of nobility, such as would distinguish a god if gods were any longer possible.

I should add that it's easy to fault Stevens' generalisations here as elsewhere. If indeed the idea of God dominated the poetry of the past, surely the poetry of nature and of secular love rivalled it. Neither does it seem to me evident that the modern imagination today is universally moving away from God; on the contrary, religion, especially fundamentalist religion, has become a source of such murderous sectarian violence in the Middle East as has not been seen in the West since the 15th, 16th, 17th centuries. On a brighter note, three recent novels by Marilynne Robinson set in Gilead, a small town in Iowa, at a time when Stevens was at his acme as a poet, serve as convincing evidence that, at least in America, the Bible is as central to as many people's lives and beliefs as it ever was. But never mind what Stevens claimed in his sometimes fascinating, sometimes infuriating polemics; let's look at two or three of his poems after a word or two about Stevens himself.

Wallace Stevens was born into a prosperous lawyer's family in Reading, Pennsylvania, as long ago as 1879. Educated at Harvard and the New York Law School, he matured to live through some of the 20th century's most discomforting ills and anxieties: the Depression, the great drought in the American west, mass unemployment and starvation, the ascension to power of Hitler and Stalin, the Holocaust, the horrors of World War II into which the United States was catapulted by the Japanese attack on Pearl Harbour, followed by that giant step forward in mankind's capacity to kill brought about by the atomic bomb. It is easy to guess, even after a few glances at Stevens' poetry, that the violent disequilibrium of his time encouraged his essentially romantic, joy-seeking, truth-loving passion for philosophy and poetry to disengage from the violent turmoil of ideological politics and, in its 'rage for order', concern itself with ideas about how imagination might convert the uncontrollable realities of life into art. Although contemporary with Pound, Eliot and the major modernists, Stevens avoided a literary milieu both in academia and in New York and led a double life as a poet and successful businessman in Hartford, Connecticut. By day he went to work in a suit and tie as an executive of the Hartford Accident and Indemnity Company. By night he retired to his study to indulge his ideas and write his poetry. Apart from yearly holidays in Florida, he travelled only in his mind. Though he read voluminously in French, German and the classics, he never ventured abroad. He never even strayed from the East Coast of the United States. When he died aged 75 in 1955, he had won a Pulitzer Prize and two National Book Awards and was acknowledged as a major figure in American letters. Today our populist and personality oriented literary world has turned the elitist ideas of the modernists out of doors. And though Wallace Stevens is still a name, his poetry is neither popular nor understood, which is why I want to look at these particular poems this evening.

I have said that, apart from his philosophical objections to believing in God, Stevens was a religious poet in the Anglo-American tradition. By this I mean that his relationship with the idea he called a supreme fiction was not exclusively abstract or even philosophical. He was intimate with it in much the same way that George Herbert was intimate with his 'dear angry Lord'. Compare the tone and language of Stevens' introduction to 'Notes toward a Supreme Fiction' with Herbert's famous and beloved dialogue, 'Love'. Here is Stevens:

> And for what, except for you, do I feel love?
> Do I press the extremist book of the wisest man
> Close to me, hidden in me day and night?
> In the uncertain light of single, certain truth,
> Equal in living changingness to the light
> In which I meet you, in which we sit at rest,
> For a moment in the central of our being,
> The vivid transparence that you bring is peace.[5]

And here, Herbert:

> Love bade me welcome: yet my soul drew back,
>> Guiltie of dust and sinne.
> But quick-ey'd Love, observing me grow slack
>> From my first entrance in,
> Drew nearer to me, sweetly questioning,
>> If I lack'd anything.
>
> A guest, I answer'd, worthy to be here:
>> Love said, You shall be he.
> I the unkinde, ungratefull? Ah my deare,
>> I cannot look on thee.
> Love took my hand, and smiling did reply,
>> Who made the eyes but I?
>
> Truth, Lord, but I have marr'd them: let my shame
>> Go where it doth deserve.
> And know you not, sayes Love, who bore the blame?
>> My deare, then I will serve.
> You must sit down, sayes Love, and taste my meat:
>> So I did sit and eat.[6]

Separated by four hundred years and speaking out from different countries, historical periods and beliefs, the writers of these poems shared a language, a tone of voice – modest, even humble – yet secure in the common dignity (nobility) of their personalities. Stevens himself proffered in *The Necessary Angel* a possible definition of poetry as a process of the personality of the poet. By which he did not mean that it involves the poet as subject but that the writing of a lasting poem has to be the act of a living mind that imprints itself unforgettably on its sounds and rhythms. Apart from the times and places in which they were written, the chief differences between these two well-known, unforgettable poems have to do with (1) form; Herbert is a master of rhymed pentameter in a regulated pattern whereas Stevens writes here in flexible blank verse; and (2) faith that in Herbert's case is never in doubt, whereas Stevens allows an oxymoron to give his ambiguous faith the breath of life he called reality. 'In the *uncertain* light of single *certain* truth / Equal in living *changingness* to the light' suggests the paintings by Cézanne and Paul Klee Stevens so admired. Herbert, of course, would never have given voice to religious doubts, although it could be that he sometimes wrote poems to conquer them.

Those eight lines introducing 'Notes toward a Supreme Fiction' should look familiar; Stevens wanted to prepare his reader for embarkation on a long philosophical poem with an invocation to his muse. Note, though, that his eleven syllable first line is more at ease than Milton's opening of *Paradise Lost*, which so arrestingly wrenches that great poem open. They are even more orderly than the first line of Herbert's 'Love'. Compare the smooth flow of 'And for *what* except for *you* do *I feel love?*' with the violent eruption of 'Of **man's first** diso**be**dience and the **fruit** / Of that for**bid**den **tree** whose **mor**tal **taste** / brought **death** into our **world** and all our **woe**...' and then with the relaxed pattern of stresses stretched over ten syllables in '*Love* bade me *wel*come: [breath] yet my *soul drew back*...' Iambic pentameter is a wonderfully flexible metre, as many poets since Shakespeare and Milton have discovered.

Note, too, how Stevens, a master of rhythms, chose to surprise us in his opening lines by directly addressing a 'what' and not a 'whom'. A muse? An angel? Either figure could stand for the imaginative power of the writer's mind, source of that supreme fiction, which Stevens believed to be as close as we ever get to any transcendent truth. Whatever 'what' is in this poem, it is above all things desirable and necessary, a condition of the human spirit that admits of a perfect receptivity known to saints, mystics and poets (as indeed to George Herbert) as the happiest condition of consciousness – which is why Stevens' iambic rhythm remains unruffled. The 'what' in the first line later becomes a 'you' and finally a 'we' as perfect love between the poet and the spirit of poetry is consummated in perfect peace. I am reminded of Seamus Heaney's 'The Harvest Bow' and the quotation at the end: *The end of art is peace*.[7]

The main body of the poem 'Notes toward a Supreme Fiction' is too long to treat with fewer than hours of study in hand. Suffice it to say that it undertakes to strip both religion and art down to a first element – 'the idea of the sun', which for Stevens was the origin of nature, mankind and the idea of God, which now must serve as the original source of a nameless 'nobility' of mind. 'The death of one god is the death of all [...] But Phoebus was / A name for something that never could be named. / There was a project for the sun and is [...] The sun / Must bear no name, gold flourisher, but be/ In the difficulty of what it is to be.'[8]

Well, I confess I'm rather fond of all this finding words to say there are no words for God. I can't believe that Stevens wasn't enjoying himself, playing with ideas. It will profit us more, though, to look at 'Sunday Morning', one of his first published poems dating from the time of World War I, when Stevens was still under the spell of the 19th-century Romantics. Compare the sounds and rhythms of this poem (available in any edition of Stevens' poems; I can reprint no more of it than the last stanzas) with the language of Wordsworth's 'Immortality Ode' to see how, in 'Sunday Morning' Stevens argues just the opposite case. For him there is no such thing as personal immortality; we must content ourselves with the glories of the earth.

> We live in an old chaos of the sun,
> Or old dependency of day and night, [...]
> Deer walk upon our mountains, and the quail
> Whistle about us their spontaneous cries;
> Sweet berries ripen in the wilderness;
> And in the isolation of the sky,
> At evening, casual flocks of pigeons make
> Ambiguous undulations as they sink,
> Downward to darkness, on extended wings.[9]

'Sunday Morning' seems to me now, as it did when I met it as a student, one of the most beautiful-sounding, rich, musical and, in Steven's word, 'noble' expressions of spiritual *unfaith* in the canon. It sits there calmly near the centre of American literature, together with passages from Thoreau's *Walden* and Whitman's *Leaves of Grass*, challenging the nervous lines of Wordsworth's 'Intimations of Immortality'. To me, 'Sunday Morning' is more convincing. For a comparable epiphany in Wordsworth's canon, turn to his sonnet 'Upon Westminster Bridge' in which the revelation is achieved without strain.

As it happened, 'Sunday Morning', beautiful as it is, was a one-off. It was too lush, too romantic both in subject and style, for Stevens to want to repeat the performance. He needed contemporary language to explore contemporary ideas and evolve a style that answered the demands of the new wave in the arts that followed the First World War. The poems for which he is today either adored or ignored 'make it new' with a vengeance, mixing ebullient philosophy with spectacular word play – their titles often as intriguing as the poems they head: 'The Snow Man', 'Le Monocle de Mon Oncle', 'Anecdote of the Jar', 'Peter Quince at the Clavier', 'The Man with the Blue Guitar', 'Thirteen Ways of Looking at a Blackbird', 'Esthétique du Mal'. No one could claim that any of these were written in the tradition of Herbert or Wordsworth or even Yeats. Nevertheless, I contend that when Wallace Stevens forgot to play with words as an artist plays with paints and colours, when he stopped theorising in the abstract and listened to the poetry singing in his ears, he returned to the lyric harmony that had seduced him in the first place. He called his first published book *Harmonium*. Towards the end of his life, he proposed calling his *Collected Poems, The Whole of Harmonium*.

This is why I want, as a gesture towards Stevens as the figure of the 'noble' American poet, to turn to a poem of his that I think bears more of his true *inscape* (a word coined by Hopkins) than 'Sunday Morning'. I first warmed to this poem when I heard Adrienne Rich read it on the radio about forty years ago when I was living in Cambridge, Massachusetts. She introduced it as a poem about reading she would never tire of hearing, and it has since that evening been numbered among my epiphanies.

The House Was Quiet and the World Was Calm

The house was quiet and the world was calm.
The reader became the book; and summer night

Was like the conscious being of the book.
The house was quiet and the world was calm.

The words were spoken as if there was no book,
Except that the reader leaned above the page,

Wanted to lean, wanted much most to be
The scholar to whom his book is true, to whom

The summer night is like a perfection of thought.
The house was quiet because it had to be.

The quiet was part of the meaning, part of the mind:
The access of perfection to the page.

And the world was calm. The truth in a calm world,
In which there is no other meaning, itself

Is calm, itself is summer and night, itself
Is the reader leaning late and reading there.[10]

What can we say about such a poem to describe or explain its distinction? Several things. To begin with, we notice that it avoids the embarrassment of a first person narrator; neither author nor persona takes an active part in it. This, I should add, is Stevens' normal practice; so rarely does he take part personally in his own poems that when he does – as in the Introduction to 'Notes toward a Supreme Fiction' – we are taken aback. In 'Sunday Morning' the presiding persona is a woman – a female personification of Stevens himself, or perhaps a woman Stevens knew or imagined. It hardly matters. 'The House Was Quiet' in contrast, opens with a set of verbs in the passive mood. The reader at the centre is not the speaker; he is someone who has been acted upon: the house was quiet, the world was calm, the words were spoken. Not until the sixth line, after the word 'Except', does the reader act (still in the past tense) by leaning above the page, willing him or her self to become 'the scholar to whom the book is true'. The word 'true' alerts us to an impending mystery brought about by the calm of the summer night, which allows for an encounter with perfection: 'it is like a perfection of thought'. We then return to the image of the house, 'quiet because it had to be. / The quiet was part of the meaning, part of the mind,' before the line, 'The access of perfection to the page' brings the book back into the picture. And now the reader, the book, the house and the calm world, like the many-way fusion of dots in a pointillist painting, seem to be enveloped by a unity of being – Stevens' truth. We have already encountered truth in those lines prefacing 'Notes toward a Supreme Fiction': 'In the uncertain light of single certain truth / Equal in living changingness to the light.'

To my mind, both poems represent in the simplest language moments of epiphany, which are just as mysterious, or even more mysterious, than feelings we might have been taught to articulate in prayer. Yet Stevens' language makes the experience of holiness feel as inevitable as miraculous: 'The truth in a calm world / in which there is no other meaning, itself / is calm, itself is summer and night, itself / is the reader leaning late and reading there.' The revelation at the end, you'll notice, is still received in the passive mood, though now in the present tense, a tense that also implies limitless duration.

To me, as to Adrienne Rich, 'The House Was Quiet and the World Was Calm' is Wallace Stevens at his most moving. It illustrates, too, his theory of reality and imagination (a dominant idea behind all his poetry) better, I think, than the philosophising stanzas of long poems such as 'Notes toward a Supreme Fiction' and 'An Ordinary Evening in New Haven' and more convincingly than poems like 'The Man with the Blue Guitar', which apes the techniques of Picasso, Klee and other painters Stevens admired.

A few more examples will help fill out this personal and incomplete overview of Stevens' epiphanies. Among the most mysterious and beautiful poems in *The Rock*, Stevens' last, unfinished book, is 'The World as Meditation',[11] which again summons the spirit of poetry as an imaginary Penelope meditates on the return of Ulysses. Or is she a personification of spring after a long winter meditating on the return of the sun? Or both? Here, once again, is a woman – let's call her poetry's or the poet's soul – who apprehends the coming of the spirit of life, the necessary angel, in the heroic rising of the sun. Some absolute yet intimate relationship between artist, the sun and life itself fuels the continual meditation that underlies the unceasing human endeavour to create. The poem celebrates the marriage of the artist with the earth and its seasons as they endlessly revolve in the changing yet unchanging light. I suspect for Stevens, as for Georges Enesco, from whose journal he quotes in the prefatory introduction to this poem, meditation was a form of continual secular prayer.

Finally, let me draw your attention to an early poem and then to two late ones in which Stevens reflects on his life's work. Each of his books can be understood as movements in a single composition, a symphony of sorts in which themes recur again and again. One repeated motif is that nothing material exists for us humans but the world we inhabit, our imagination's idea of ordinary reality – the ever-changing reality, in short, of conditions we have to accept. 'The Death of a Soldier',[12] an early poem written during World War I, expresses a naturalist's faith in the finality of death. The entire poem consists of a stoic epitaph, which ends bluntly –

Death is absolute and without memorial,
As in a season of autumn,
When the wind stops,

When the wind stops and, over the heavens,
The clouds go, nevertheless,
In their direction.

One can follow Stevens' elaborations of this centrally grim theme as he develops out of it a compensatory theory of imagination in his later work, arguing that the shaping of reality through imagination is art's principal obligation and joy. The poet's imagination is that which opposes and 'presses against' reality, he wrote in *The Necessary Angel*, to create in the mind of the poet-seer, or, indeed, of any truly enlightened witness, visions of beautiful and unattainable perfection. This imaginary glimpse of perfection or truth is all Stevens desired of heaven. You can see how this idea relates to all the poems we have considered this evening, as it does to a late poem, 'Of Mere Being',[13] which depicts a state of transcendence or 'vivid transparence' that eludes reality's seductive worldly offerings – power, say, or fame – by uniting the artist with a vision of 'the palm at the end of the mind' rising in the 'bronze distance', together with a gold-feathered bird that sings in its branches a song meaningless to man and his feelings. It is similar to the artificial bird 'of hammered gold and gold enamelling' in Yeats' poem, 'Sailing to Byzantium', except that Stevens' is the more wonderful for being self-created in the mind of the artist rather than produced by a goldsmith for the entertainment of an emperor and his court.

There is, of course, far more to say about the poems of Wallace Stevens than I have been able to touch on this evening. But I hope you will at least have caught a glimpse of the profound poet behind the facade of ornamental fancy work in which he hid himself much of the time. His own assessment of his poetic life as a brief participator in the life of the planet is stated modestly in his late poem called 'The Planet on the Table'.[14] I shall finish by letting Stevens have the last word as to why he, self-titled Ariel (and perhaps suggesting the name to Sylvia Plath, who admired him), was glad he had had a share in the sun long enough to have written his poems.

Ariel was glad he had written his poems.
They were of a remembered time
Or of something seen that he liked.

[...]
It was not important that they survive.
What mattered was that they should bear
Some lineament or character,

Some affluence, if only half perceived,
In the poverty of their words,
Of the planet of which they were part.

NOTE: For reasons of copyright I have had to omit the text of several relevant poems included in the original talk. References to their sources can be found in the notes at the back of the book.

Sylvia Plath: The Illusion of a Greek Necessity

It is now over 50 years since Sylvia Plath died at 30 in London, never knowing she was about to become the pivotal, most influential woman poet of the 20th century. In 'Edge', which was probably her last poem, she sees herself (or a persona like herself) lying dead, like a classical statue, the heroine/victim of 'the illusion of a Greek necessity.' Twenty-five years ago, when I was completing *Bitter Fame*, my biography of Plath, I tried to play down the element of victimhood in the popular myth that flourished in many quarters after her death. This was because throughout the 1980s and 90s, the official feminist take on Plath's suicide was to see her as the "victim" of Ted Hughes' adultery and male-privileged desertion. From what I had read and heard from various witnesses of their marriage breakup and its final repercussions in the suicide of Assia Wevill (who, with herself, gassed her daughter by Ted), I found it impossible to believe any explanation so simple as that Ted Hughes, by all accounts a man who valued Sylvia's genius and sacrificed much to it, would wilfully abandon the mother of his children, a person he regarded as a major poet, simply because he had fallen in love with another woman. Such a scenario, out of *True Romances* or some cheap novel, couldn't and wouldn't do for any of this tragedy's *dramatis personae*. Since writing my book, however, I have thought a good deal about Sylvia Plath's alleged victimhood, concluding, finally, that I do think she was – as she saw herself in 'Edge' and other late poems – a victim, but certainly not of Ted Hughes nor really of any individual – neither of her mother nor her father. She was not even a victim of her beloved psychotherapist, Ruth Beuscher, whose well-meaning but sadly unprofessional advice she came to depend on. I believe, in short, that Sylvia Plath was a victim of her own brilliantly imaginative brain, which was probably irrevocably damaged when, in the summer of 1953, sleepless and fearful of going mad, she was given, as an outpatient, electroconvulsive therapy (ECT) by a careless or incompetent psychiatrist in a run-of-the-mill Massachusetts mental home. In this, I believe, she was tragically a victim of a time when ECT was considered an efficient and effective psychoanalytical practice.

There is little doubt that Sylvia Plath's treatment by electrolysis led directly to her decision to commit suicide; as she wrote after her attempt to a friend, Eddie Cohen, 'The only alternative I could see was an eternity of hell for the rest of my life in a mental hospital, and I was going to make use of my last ounce of free choice and choose a quick, clean ending.' The story of Plath's failed suicide and slow recovery at 20, later supplied her with the plot of her only novel, *The Bell Jar*, and is certainly the spark which set alight many of her most powerful poems.

All Plath's work, at source, is autobiographical, but instead of celebrating epiphanies of visionary experience or invoking moments of profound emotion, like Wordsworth's or Dylan Thomas's, it mostly consists of fragmented stages of symbolic, often frantic, self-exploration. The kind of poetry Plath initiated – and not, I think, the kind she wished to be remembered by – is a poetry that continually balances on the thin line between art and psychotherapy.

Such an approach – especially attractive to her (and my) generation of Americans – has appealed to women as no other form of poetry ever has before. Up to the middle 1950s, writing poetry was chiefly a male prerogative; apart from Emily Brontë, Emily Dickinson, maybe Edna St Vincent Millay, few women poets were considered worthy of inclusion in the college anthologies. Marianne Moore and Elizabeth Bishop were, like Wallace Stevens, acceptable as "modernists" on the model of T.S. Eliot – which is to say, experimental and deliberately impersonal. Both felt insulted when reviewed as women poets. Elizabeth

Bishop famously refused to allow her poems to appear in all-women anthologies.

With the sudden emergence of Sylvia Plath, Anne Sexton and a number of other extremist poets in the 1960s, all this changed. A whole new category of "confessional poetry" appeared, as if conjured from the heady atmosphere of rebellion and self-doubt many of us felt who graduated from colleges in the United States to become wives and mothers, having been educated to expect lives very different from those of our mothers and grandmothers. My own contribution to the literature of confession was a long epistolary poem, *Correspondences*, written in the 1970s, ten years after Sylvia Plath's death, in which I tried to give the movement a background in American social history by inventing a family something like my own (but not my own) in whose names I wrote letters modelled on letters I'd discovered in my family archive. These I augmented by borrowings from 19th century letters I found in the archives of the Schlesinger Library at Harvard. As I look back on the writing of *Correspondences*, I see it partly as an attempt to broaden and deepen the scope of the confessional movement, partly as an attempt to discourage young poets – especially women – from writing exclusively and obsessively about their selves.

Surprised to have survived those turbulent years, I now look back to the period spanning the 1960s and 70s as a time of prolonged cultural adolescence when many young women in the West discovered in themselves hormones of unconscious cravings for which they had never before found common language. Sylvia Plath's *Ariel*, when it appeared in 1965, was timed perfectly to galvanise the women's movement into action, encouraging many a bright, ambitious girl on the verge of adulthood to idolise or imitate this uniquely gifted American whose self-imprisonment and psychic polarisation forced her to succeed at killing herself at 30 where she had failed at 20. Today, 50 years after her death, it is time we took seriously what Ted Hughes had to say about the enormous human cost of Plath's poetry.

Ted Hughes and Ted Hughes alone, was witness – hour after hour, day after day, week after week for six years – to 'the birth circumstances' of Sylvia Plath's poems, to the astonishing rapidity of her maturation as an artist, and to how, as her style sharpened, she struggled to overcome the demands of the deadly myth – that 'great, stark, bloody play' she could not help writing in the ever-narrowing psychological space behind the facade of her, on the whole, privileged daily life. Alone among her contemporaries, Hughes understood the extremes, positive and negative, between which, to use her own word, Plath helplessly 'ricocheted'. He patiently supported, often at the cost of his own work, the courageous toil that kept at bay the death – that black threatening alternative to brilliant performance – that Plath's poems tell us was always close at hand. It is of a helplessly trapped, fiercely combatant spirit that Hughes wrote, in an essay on her journals,

> Sylvia Plath's poetry, like a species on its own, exists in little else but the revelation of that birth and purpose. Although her whole considerable ambition was fixed on becoming the normal flowering and fruiting kind of writer, her work was roots only. Almost as if her entire oeuvre were enclosed within those processes and transformations that happen in other poets before they can even begin [...] Or as if all poetry were made up of the feats and shows performed by the poetic spirit Ariel. Whereas her poetry is the biology of Ariel, the ontology of Ariel – the story of Ariel's imprisonment in the pine, before Prospero opened it.[1]

Hughes' last collection of poems, *Birthday Letters* (1998), bears witness to the evolution of Plath's poetry from the time of their meeting in February 1956 to her death in February 1963. It is at once a book of poems and a series of investigations into their partnership, supporting, if I may say so, my contention in *Bitter Fame*, that Hughes battled for many years against his wife's destructive polarities but failed at last to free either her or himself from their spell. After her death, despite aggressive attacks on himself and the repeated desecration of Plath's grave in Heptonstall, where she was buried under her married name, Hughes set himself soberly to trace and analyse Plath's growth as a poet in a series of insightful introductions to her work.

Now that Plath's original selection for her volume, *Ariel*, has been published,[2] there is all the more reason to listen to Hughes's reasons for making the selection he did for the edition of 1965. I hope that comparisons between the two versions will help to heal, not inflame, the hatred generated after her death – chiefly by people, stunned by the power of her poetry, but who did not know her, or knew her only superficially. In any case, all Plath's poems were made available to the public in the chronological order of their writing in *The Collected Poems*, published by Faber in 1981.[2] Having re-read them for the purposes of this talk, I have been impressed all over again by their beauty, their persuasiveness, their grit and rhythmic invention, yet I am more than ever disturbed by their build-up of concentrated anguish, malice and aggression. As before, I can't help but conclude that the strongest of Plath's poems have to be understood as paradoxical. As a body of work, they tell us how an exceptionally gifted poet fought for her life by again and again dwelling on the lurid particulars of her death; nearly every poem in *Ariel* is a bid for survival by dying, and like Lady Lazarus, doing it 'exceptionally well' – well enough, anyway, to deserve being born again, stepping from 'the black car of Lethe/ Pure as a baby'. (See 'Getting There', *CP*, p.249.)

Such a contradiction can only be explained as her doctor, Dr Horder, in great distress, explained it much later. 'I believe', he wrote, 'that she was liable to large swings of mood, but so excessive that a doctor inevitably thinks in terms of brain chemistry. This does not reduce the concurrent importance of marriage breakup or of exhaustion after a period of unusual artistic activity or from recent infectious illnesses or from the difficulties of being a responsible, practical mother. The full explanation has to take all these factors into account and more. But the irrational compulsion to end it all makes me think that the body was governing the mind.' Proof of an insane suicidal logic lay in the care with which she sealed the room where her two small children were sleeping, setting out bread and milk for them, and in the note she left for the nurse due to arrive in the morning, 'Please call Dr Horder' with his telephone number.[4]

Sylvia Plath would hardly be the iconic figure that she is today if she had simply written some fine poems and then, in period of sleepless insanity, killed herself. Nor, had her tragedy not been reflective of her time, would she be today the most celebrated poet of her generation, which is why for an epigraph to the Epilogue of *Bitter Fame*, I chose this quote from an essay by Joyce Carol Oates called 'The Death Throes of Romanticism'.

> Tragedy is not a woman, however gifted, dragging her shadow around in a circle, or analysing with dazzling scrupulosity the stale, boring inertia of the circle; tragedy is cultural, mysteriously enlarging the individual so that what he has experienced is both what we have experienced and what we need not experience – because of his, or her, private agony. It is proper to say that Sylvia Plath represents for us a tragic figure involved in a tragic action and that her tragedy is offered to us as a near-perfect work of art, in her books.

Yes, I think, proper and true. It is well to consider that the self-conflict and madness that led Sylvia Plath to suicide were not singular to her, not wholly personal in the self-centred self-manufactured sense they appear to be in her poems; they were hallmarks of the tragedy that engulfed much of the world in the early decades of the 20th century. Madness lay behind the multiple causes of two World Wars, behind nuclear technologies for dealing out death to millions, behind refined techniques of torture and mass murder in the Lagers of the Nazis and the Gulags of the Soviet Union. The suffering, the inhumanity and the real craziness of a brutalised Europe found expression in the counter-madness of Modern Art – in Dadaism, Cubism, Vorticism, Futurism, Abstract Expressionism – to which Sylvia Plath, with a poet's sensitivity to atmosphere, responded with the verbal energy and punch she brought to all her writing. In her late poems, she never hesitated to conflate her extreme state of suffering with that of a Jewish victim of the Holocaust. But even in 1956, the tidy stanzas of the love poems she wrote in Cambridge after she met Ted Hughes are slung out in a violent language of exalted persecution. Here are the first lines of 'Pursuit' (*CP*, p. 22).

> There is a panther stalks me down:
> One day I'll have my death of him;
> His greed has set the woods aflame,
> He prowls more lordly than the sun.
> Most soft, most suavely glides that step,
> Advancing always at my back;
> From gaunt hemlock, rooks croak havoc:

Already Plath had developed a language of startling cacophony: hemlock, rooks, croak, havoc, trek, rocks, wakes. Crackling sounds like these were to serve her well in her mature work. It now seems inevitable that in second half of the 20th century Sylvia Plath and Ted Hughes between them would do much to change the direction and character of poetry in the English language. In this, of course, they were not alone. They were contemporary with Ginsberg and the Beat Generation in America; and Plath was for a while, with Anne Sexton, a student of Robert Lowell whose openly confessional poetry served them both as a models. For when Ted and Sylvia met in Cambridge early in 1956, fashionable verse, in both their countries, had, as if in retreat from the savage inhumanity of the war, deliberately civilised itself in tone and form. In Britain, poetry took to a kind of neo-Georgian elegance; Robert Conquest's The Movement confirmed the conservatism of Philip Larkin's metrical irony and cynical despair. In the United States a measured, plain-spoken approach to natural philosophy (I suppose you could call it) found a model in Robert Frost, whose infectious example inspired the generation that benefited from the GI (education) Bill, producing in the 1950s the highly polished stanzas of among others, Richard Wilbur, Anthony Hecht and (well before feminism) Plath's early arch-rival, Adrienne Cecile Rich.

Before Sylvia met Ted Hughes, she assumed that she would continue to write in the manner of her college models, W.H. Auden and Richard Wilbur. Her background in middle-class Wellesley was, for all her German heritage, suburban-American to the core, steeped in the values of individualism and responsibility for personal success. From her early journals we learn how hard Sylvia Plath worked to achieve this all-important success, while all the time she was suppressing – as she came to realise – an 'other' highly conflicted inner self, a debilitating double, a chthonic figure of darkness and desire for extinction which, even in her school days, undermined her, pulling her down into pits of despair as she climbed publicly from triumph to triumph. So it happened that this lively, highly competitive, attractive American girl, so gifted, so ambitious, so happy, went off one summer to New York to be a student editor of a fashion magazine and returned two weeks later to bury herself in a crawl space under her house and swallow sleeping pills until she lost consciousness.

It seems that Sylvia Plath's failure to achieve death, aged 20, preceded by an outpatient's course of crudely administered electric shock treatments, stunned her at a point of development she never outgrew, just as the process of her lingering 'rebirth' in McLean's Sanatorium, near Boston, confirmed her illusion that dying was a necessary prelude to being born again. Such is the plot of *The Bell Jar*, complete with its heroine's subjection to ECT and the killing off of a threatening female double before she can recover. The novel ends with the heroine returning to college 'patched for the road' like a repaired tyre, as if the author (whom we know has been the real heroine all along) realised that in the deep underworld of her psyche her other self, that evil, death-dealing double, had been temporarily satisfied but not vanquished.

Given the shape and structure of this controlling myth, Dr Ruth Beuscher, the young psychotherapist who won Plath's confidence after her suicide attempt, leaped to the conclusion that Sylvia's breakdown had originated with the death of her father when she was eight. Plath eagerly grasped at this Freudian analysis (whether for the first time, we do not know; no sign appears in the journals before the summer of her suicide attempt in 1953 that she excessively missed her father), claiming for herself an Electra Complex, and making use of it again and again in a sequence of poems that never seemed to lay Otto

Plath to rest or to cure her permanently of her yearning to join him.

Part of the reason for Sylvia Plath's inability to abandon her identification with Electra must be laid at the door of the times and the pervasiveness all over America in the latter 20th century of psychoanalysis as an unquestionable faith, almost a religion. With ancient Greek and fertility myths cited as universal archetypes by both Freud and Jung, thousands of sensitive young Americans, fearful of failure (in America, failure is often regarded as a secular sin), took themselves off to psychiatrists for spiritual rehabilitation. Dr Beuscher, fascinated by her brilliant patient, established a hold over her by suggesting that both her husband and her mother might be possible 'enemies'. If we are to believe Plath's journal of 1959, Dr Beuscher on one occasion openly gave Sylvia 'permission to hate her mother' – apparently never hesitating to suggest to her vivid imagination the image of a classically martyred queen who turns up years later, triumphantly dead in that late, terrifying poem 'Edge' (*CP*, p. 272).

> The woman is perfected.
> Her dead
>
> Body wears the smile of accomplishment,
> The illusion of a Greek necessity
>
> Flows in the scroll of her toga [...]

Note the word 'illusion' in connection with 'necessity', as if the poet knew, even on the threshold of her suicide, that she was acting out a myth. And how strange that this double who is previewing her death, is wearing a toga, the garment of a Roman senator, not the flowing robe of a Greek goddess.

Evidently, Sylvia Plath never forgot any therapeutic suggestion that related to or magnified her plight. Terrified, even as a child, of not being loved and praised enough, of not succeeding in pleasing her mother in everything she undertook to do, and especially of not realising in the actual world of experience, the beautiful world of her Apollonian dreams, Sylvia Plath, emerging into adulthood, let her imagination play over images of death in connection with her father while at the same time inventing for herself a number of threatening doubles, rivals, and competitors – all women like her mother, who had to be 'killed' before Sylvia could be born again. There was really no room for anyone in her Freudian Family Romance that was not a manifestation of herself or of the father who had 'deserted' her by dying, or of the mother who poisoned her love by her anxious hovering. Poor Aurelia Plath became for her daughter the archetypal betrayer whose worrisome devotion Sylvia, in the end, had had to reject as the indictment of a false saint. The vicious poem, 'Medusa', is surely an attempt to rid herself finally of this familial demon who, ten years earlier, had delivered her daughter to the torturer who maimed her permanently by subjecting her to electro-convulsive therapy. (See 'Medusa', *CP*, p. 224.)

Reading this poem against the background of Sylvia's fury at the time – a fury not only with her husband but with her entire life and fate – we can guess that the line 'Bottle in which I live' refers as much to the glass womb of her own bell-jar as to the body of her unfortunate mother. And yet, Plath's poems to her baby son, written in the same month, revert to the imagery of her beautiful poem, 'Candles' (*CP*, p. 148), written in London in 1960, for her new born daughter. Candles and candlelight must have represented a kind of salvation to her, or at least the peace and gentleness of what might be a believable Christian answer to her anguished cries. In any case, the courageous fight she put up almost daily to escape from her pine tree (or mother's womb or bell jar) to become, in Hughes's words, 'a normal flowering and fruiting writer' had found a language of hope in 'Candles' that she was never able returned to.

'Candles' is a rarity among Plath's poems because the confessional mode fits it so beautifully, and yet it opens generously to the universal. Every mother who has ever nursed a tiny baby at midnight can identify with its speaker's calm tone of fulfilment. The lines, 'How shall I tell anything at all / To this infant still in a birth drowse' are unforgettable. Yet even here, disturbing images obtrude: 'the bald moon', the 'nun-souled' candles that 'never marry'. In contrast, the terror of what Plath remembered as near electrocution before her suicide attempt resurfaced during that first pregnancy in the six snapping lines of 'The Hanging Man'. (*CP*, p. 141) Apparently that nightmare was never far away.

In October of the same year, 1960, on the day before she wrote 'Candles', Sylvia wrote a strange poem called 'Love Letter' (*CP*, p. 147), seemingly addressed to Dr Beuscher, replaying the miracle she achieved by bringing Sylvia back to life when, like a stone, she lay 'dead and unbothered by it'. The word, 'stone', recalls 'The Stones' (*CP*, p. 136) from 'Poem for a Birthday', written a year earlier, in October, 1959, a calculated, 'mad' account of her transformations in the underworld of electro-convulsive therapy, followed by her resurrection in the never-never land of McLean hospital.

> Here they can doctor heads, or any limb.
> On Fridays the little children come
>
> To trade their hooks for hands.
> Dead men leave eyes for others.
> Love is the uniform of my bald nurse.
>
> Love is the bone and sinew of my curse.
> The vase, reconstructed, houses
> The elusive rose.

Unexpectedly, in the week of her 27th birthday at Yaddo Writers' Colony in New York, Plath's Ariel voice had tried out these first astonishing cadences. Exactly a year later 'Love Letter' appeared, yet another poem which describes a 'dead' speaker's return to life as she 'started to bud like a March twig; / An arm and a leg, an arm, a leg', ascending from 'stone to cloud like a sort of god'. It suggests that neither the brisk stanzas of 'The Hanging Man' nor the soothing cadences of 'Candles' could do away with Plath's conviction that she had to undergo physical death before she could enter a new phase of creative life. A violent quarrel with her husband, followed by a miscarriage in February 1961, prompted a poem of deep depression, 'Parliament Hill Fields' (*CP*, p. 152), followed by a bitter poem on marriage, 'Zoo Keeper's Wife' (*CP*, p. 154). Soon after came 'Morning Song' (*CP*, p. 156), usually taken to be a paeon in praise of childbirth. For all the finesse of its imagery and language, I find it chilling. Until the final lines, not a single image from life gives her newborn baby human flesh and blood. The child is compared first with a gold watch; then its footsoles (not feet) are slapped and a 'bald cry' takes its place among the elements. The baby is a statue in a draughty museum, its parents are walls, and the mother is no more than a cloud distilling a mirror to reflect it own disappearance. If Plath had been a philosophical materialist, such images might have been expected. Here, they surely reflect incipient depression. Even when the baby's cry pulls the mother from bed 'cow-heavy and floral' in her Victorian nightgown, the baby remains remote, opening its mouth like a cat before trying its 'handful of notes'. The only sign of joy or hope seems to be that the baby's 'notes' rising like balloons – anticipating that amusing singleton among Plath's last poems called 'Balloons' (*CP*, p. 271).

All the poems of 1960, 1961, written in London before the Hughes found a home in rural Devon, are slung out with a characteristic mixture of vulnerability and toughness: Plathian words: bald, stone, bandage, hospital, mirror, pond, echoes, museum, hooks surface again and again – particularly the word 'bald', associated indiscriminately with the moon, with a nurse, with cries, with eyes – its origin probably the image of her father's drowning skull. Best known among these London poems, 'In Plaster' and 'Tulips' (*CP*, p. 158 & 160) were stimulated by an appendectomy Plath underwent in St Pancras Hospital in February 1961. The tough-talking 'In Plaster' offers readers a detached half-amused analysis of a schizoid condition; 'Tulips' expresses Plath's recurring desire for extinction or self-effacement. Between them, these two finely tuned, half-deadly poems were powerful enough to raise their author's state of mind once again from deep depression and restore it to a state of enthusiasm, energy and self-confidence. Still, both poems forecast what was to come. When, in late August, 1961, she moved with Ted Hughes and their baby to Court Green in North Tawton, her mind was primed and her craft honed to confront the challenge of her interior mythology as never before.

At first, after moving to Devon, Sylvia wrote nothing but enthusiastic letters to her mother and English friends, describing her beautiful house and garden and their plans for living and writing there, free of the dirt and noise of London. In view of her happy letters and cheerful neighbourhood notes in her journal, it comes as a shock to realise that one of the first and best poems Sylvia wrote at that time was 'The Moon and Yew Tree' (*CP*, p.153) at the suggestion of Ted, who, one morning, gave her as a subject the view from their bedroom window to break her writing block. He wrote later of being deeply depressed by the 'exercise' she wrote on this subject, which invoked yet again the father (yew tree) and mother (moon), phantoms of her interior mythology. As you read it, notice the colour-imagery in this poem – black tree, white moon, and the rest, blue: it's as much a surrealistic word-painting as it is a poem, depicting as hauntingly as anything by de Chirico the interior of a mind that sees death wherever it looks.

'The Moon and Yew Tree' is dated 22 October 1961. Her 29th birthday was on the 27th, five days later. Sylvia Plath by this time had explored her death theme and its counter theme, painful rebirth, in the seven parts of 'Poem for a Birthday' (*CP*, p. 131) in October 1959 and again in 'Love Letter' (*CP*, p. 147) in October, 1960. The theme recurred, with full symbolism for mother and father, in 'The Moon and Yew Tree' in October 1961. In October, 1962, she returned to it fortissimo with 'Lady Lazarus' (*CP*, p. 244), when, stunned and infuriated by her husband's adultery, after banishing him from their Devon home, she began to write the poems that made her name. Rising at four or five every morning before her babies woke, she perfected her unique voice, her Ariel voice, as she rehearsed yet again, this time triumphantly, her ineradicable interior drama. In 'Lady Lazarus', each bladed stanza had been honed and perfected over many years of practice. Nothing like it, or like any of the

Ariel poems had ever been written by a woman – or a man – before.

'Lady Lazarus' is a marvellous poem, not because of the triumphant resurrection it expresses, implying that victory is possible for the poet even after she has died in circumstances likened to the holocaust, but because of its piston-like rhythm. Its plot is Gothic, melodramatic, a woman's revenge story, but the rhythm that ties the lines together, with its almost jokey rhymes, is joyous; the poem is obviously enjoying its own performance, rushing along like a train on a track. Curiously in good poetry and certainly in the very best, content and form can effectively argue with or contradict each other. What Sylvia Plath had learned and was putting into practice in her Ariel voice was that writing a splendid poem about dying aborted her need to die. Even mournful lyrics, such as 'Mary's Song' (*CP*, p. 257) and 'The Couriers' (*CP*, p. 247), written during this wonderfully creative period (October through November of 1962) raised her spirits. Her poem to her baby son, 'Nick and the Candlestick' (*CP*, p. 240) begins with 'cold homicides' in a cave of piranha fish, but it ends with an upbeat. And here again candles, as before, are signs of blessing, of a rare, loving reconciliation with the hostile world.

Had the exultation of writing so many extraordinary poems in the space of two months lasted, Plath might well have overcome her death urge by allowing her writing persona complete creative freedom to die when it would, thus saving her actual life. But the move she made with her children in December from Devon to London interrupted the flow of her poems, and when she began to write again in January 1963, the triumphant note had disappeared. The coldest winter on record crippled England that January–February, bringing snowstorms and frozen plumbing. As Plath's spirits plummeted with the temperature, her poems, too, began abandon the struggle. Her last poems, written shortly before her suicide, such as 'Totem' and 'Edge', tell us that the airless death chamber of the bell jar had finally become lethal. If – she argued with the pseudo-rational logic of the insane – if she had 'died' at 20 and Ruth Beuscher had resurrected her and given her a new life, mightn't she die again at 30, with something like the same result? Dr Horder had found her a nurse (that 'bald' ambiguous symbol of hope); wouldn't he find a way to resurrect and return her to life, patched for the road?

Apart from her terrifying last poem, 'Edge' (*CP*, p. 272), I believe the poems that best describe Sylvia Plath's state of mind before she took her life on February 11th, 1963, are 'Totem' (*CP*, p. 264), written on January 28th, and 'Words' (*CP*, p. 270), written on February 1st. I'd like to finish by drawing them to your attention. As poems they are perfect, but as truth, they are sadly consistent with the plot of her personal drama. Her death, like her life, was a performance she couldn't escape. After her death, Ted Hughes found the perfect epigraph in the *Bhagavad Gita* to engrave on Sylvia Plath's tombstone 'Even among fierce flames, the golden lotus can be planted.'

NOTES

Poems for the Voice and Ear.
Newcastle/Bloodaxe Poetry Lectures, 23 February 2016.

1. Milan Kundera, *The Art of the Novel* (1986) as quoted in John Eliot Gardiner, *Music in the Castle of Heaven* (London: Penguin Books, 2014), 16.

2. Louise Rosenblatt, *The Reader, the Text, the Poem: The Transactional Theory of the Literary Work* (Illinois, USA: Southern Illinois University Press, 1978), 12.

3. Ibid. 12-13.

4. Francis Berry, *Poetry and the Physical Voice* (New York: Oxford University Press, 1962), 5.

5. Ibid. 7.

6. See Angela Leighton, *On Form* (Oxford: Oxford University Press, 2007), 246.

7. W.H. Auden, *The Collected Poems of W.H. Auden* (London: Random House, 1945), 48-51.

8. Angela Leighton, *On Form*, 145-46.

9. W.H. Auden, Op. Cit. 49.

10. Robert Frost, 'The Figure a Poem Makes' in *The Collected Poems* (New York: Garden City, 1942).

11. W.B. Yeats, *The Collected Poems* (London: Macmillan, 1969), 141.

12. Yeats, Ibid. 304.

13. Ibid. 'Those Dancing Days Are Gone', 302.

14. Ibid. 'Long-Legged Fly', 381.

15. Yeats, Ibid. 'Two Songs from a Play', 239.

16. *New Poets of England and America*, ed. Donald Hall, Robert Pack and Louis Simpson (New York: Meridian Books, 1957). *New Poets of England and America: Second Selection*, ed. Donald Hall and Robert Pack (New York: Meridian Books, 1962).

17. Ibid. 12.

18. Richard Wilbur, 'In the Elegy Season', Ibid. 325.

19. Richard Wilbur, 'Love Calls Us to the Things of This World'. Ibid. 328.

20. Robert Lowell, 'Mr Edwards and the Spider', Ibid. 187.

21. Richard Wilbur, 'Love Calls Us to the Things of This World'. Ibid. 328.

22. Lowell, 'Waking Early Sunday Morning' in *Near the Ocean* (London: Faber & Faber, 1967), 16.

23. Richard Wilbur, 'Love Calls Us to the Things of This World'. Ibid. 328.

The Anthology as Manifesto 1960-1980
Newcastle/Bloodaxe Poetry Lectures, 25 February 2016.

1. Donald Allen, *The New American Poetry, 1945–1960* (Berkeley, Los Angeles: University of California Press, 1960, 1999), xi.

2. Black Mountain College, founded in 1933 on the progressive educational principles of the philosopher, John Dewey, became a centre for scientific and artistic experiment, attracting, apart from its radical poets, such figures as Buckminster Fuller, John Cage, and the artist Willem de Kooning. The college, for all its innovative fame, shut down in 1957.

3. Allen, Ibid. 182-83.

4. Allen, Ibid. 244.

5. Frank O'Hara, 'Why I Am Not a Painter', *Selected Poems*, ed. Donald Allen (Carcanet Press, 2005), reprinted here in full with the permission of Carcanet Press Ltd.

6. See Anne Stevenson, *Bitter Fame*, Appendix I (London: Viking Penguin, 1989), 317.

7. Olson's 'Statement on Poetics' appears in Donald Allen, Ibid. 386-92. His version of the English lyric is on p.389. The original text is more usually given as: 'Westron wynde when wyll thow blow, / The smalle rayne downe can rayne – / Cryst, yf my love wer in my armys / And I yn my bed agayne!' (*The Oxford Book of English Verse*, ed. Christopher Ricks [Oxford: Oxford University Press, 1999], 14).

8. Ibid. 389.

9. *Literary Essays of Ezra Pound*, ed. T.S. Eliot (London: Faber & Faber, 1974), 3.

10. Theodore Roszak, *The Making of a Counter Culture* (New York: Anchor Books, Doubleday, 1969), 5-6.

11. The material in this paragraph is either derived or quoted from Stephen Greenblatt, *The Swerve: How the World Became Modern* (New York: W.W. Norton, 2011), 72-76, 199.

12. Denise Levertov, *Selected Poems* (Newcastle upon Tyne: Bloodaxe Books, 1986), 33.

13. Levertov, Ibid. 95-96.

14. See my first lecture, p. 26, and Angela Leighton, *On Form* (Oxford: Oxford University Press, 2007), 246.

15. Levertov, Ibid. 82.

What is Poetry?
Newcastle/Bloodaxe Poetry Lectures, 2 March 2016.

1. Wallace Stevens, 'The Noble Rider and the Sound of Words' in *The Necessary Angel* (New York: Vintage Books, 1942, 1951), 32

2. All the poems by G.F. Dutton are taken from *The Bare Abundance: Selected Poems 1975-2001* (Tarset: Bloodaxe Books, 2002).

3. Seamus Heaney, *North* (London: Faber & Faber, 1975), 72-73.

4. W.H. Auden, *The Enchafèd Flood* (London: Faber & Faber, 1951), 123-24.

5. Frances Horovitz, 'Rain – Birdsoswald', *Collected Poems*, ed. Roger Garfitt (Newcastle upon Tyne: Bloodaxe Books, 1985), 103.

6. Wallace Stevens, 'The Figure of the Youth as Virile Poet' in *The Necessary Angel* (NewYork: Vintage Books, 1942, 1951), 44.

7. Ibid. 45.

8. William Martin, *Lammas Alanna* (Newcastle upon Tyne: Bloodaxe Books, 2000), 128.

9. Ibid. 97-99.

10. Seamus Heaney, 'Sunlight', *North* (London: Faber & Faber, 1975), 8-9. Reproduced in full here from *Opened Ground: Poems 1966-1966* (London: Faber & Faber, 1998), by permission of Faber & Faber Ltd.

How to Read Poetry
St Chad's College, Durham University, 3 March 2013

1. Elizabeth Bishop, *The Complete Poems, 1927–1979* (London: Chatto & Windus, The Hogarth Press, 1983), 58-59.

2. Doris Kearns Goodwin, *Team of Rivals* (London: Penguin Books, 2013), 52.

3. Wade Davis, *Into the Silence: The Great War, Mallory and the Conquest of Everest* (London: Vintage Books, 2012), 507.

4. David Fuller, *The Life in the Sonnets*, in Shakespeare NOW Series, ed. Ewan Fernie and Simon Palfrey (London: Continuum International Publishing Group, 2011).

5. Ezra Pound, *Literary Essays of Ezra Pound*, ed. T.S. Eliot (London: Faber, 1954), 25.

6. Peter Redgrove, *Selected Poems* (London: Jonathan Cape, 1999), 66-67, reproduced by permission of his estate.

7. Marianne Moore, 'Poetry', *The Poems of Marianne Moore*, ed. Grace Schulman (London: Faber & Faber, 2003), 135.

8. Emily Dickinson, Poem 754 in *The Complete Poems of Emily Dickinson*, ed. Thomas H. Johnson, ed. (London: Faber & Faber, 1970), 369.

9. Robert Frost, 'Moon Compasses'. in Robert Frost, *Collected Poems, Prose & Plays* (New York: The Library of America, 1995), 273.

10. A.E. Housman, *A Shropshire Lad*, X in *The Collected Poems of A.E. Housman* (London: Jonathan Cape, 1939), 58.

5. Affinities: Robert Frost and Elizabeth Bishop
St Chad's College, Durham University, 18 March 2014

The poems of Robert Frost quoted or referred to in this talk can be found in any contemporary collection of his work. My references are all to Collected Poems, Prose, & Plays (New York: The Library of America), 1995. Elizabeth Bishop's *Complete Poems* are published in New York by Farrar, Straus and Giroux, 1983, and in Britain by Chatto & Windus, The Hogarth Press, 1983.

1. Robert Frost, Letter to John T. Bartlett in *Collected Poems, Prose, & Plays* (New York: The Library of America, 1995), 665.

2. Ibid. 'The Figure a Poem Makes', 776.

3. Ibid. 953.

4. Elizabeth Bishop, *Edgar Allan Poe & The Juke Box: Uncollected Poems, Drafts and Fragments*, ed. Alice Quinn (New York: Farrar, Straus and Giroux, 2006), 207.

5. Jay Parini, *Robert Frost: A Life* (London: William Heinemann, 1998), 444.

6. Robert Frost, Op. Cit. Library of America, 905.

7. *Notebook C*, transcribed and edited by David Kohn, 196-97, in *Charles Darwin's Notebooks, 1836-1844: Geology, Transmutation of Species, Metaphysical Enquiries*, transcribed and edited by Paul H. Barrett and others (Cambridge University Press, 1987), 300.

8. Seamus Heaney, *The Redress of Poetry* (London: Faber & Faber, 1995), 175-76.

6. Epiphanies Among the Poems of Wallace Stevens
St Chad's Chapel, Durham University, 24 February 2014

1. CENCAGE LEARNING: Gale Project, Contemporary Authors Vol. 363, ed. Mike Tyrkus (Farmington Hills, Michigan, 2015).

2. Wallace Stevens, *The Necessary Angel: Essays on Reality and the Imagination* (New York: Vintage Books, Alfred A. Knopf, 1951), 32.

3. Ibid. 33–34.

4. Wallace Stevens, *Opus Posthumous*, ed. Samuel French Morse (New York: Alfred A. Knopf, 1980), xv.

5. Wallace Stevens, *Collected Poems* (London: Faber & Faber, 2006), 331.

6. George Herbert, 'Love', in *The Oxford Book of English Verse*, ed. Christopher Ricks (Oxford: Oxford University Press, 1999), 154.

7. Seamus Heaney, *Fieldwork* (London: Faber & Faber, 1979), 58.

8. Wallace Stevens, *Collected Poems*, op.cit. 331.

9. Ibid. 61-62.

10. Ibid. 312-13.

11. Ibid. 455.

12. Ibid. 84.

13. Stevens, *Opus Posthumous*, op. cit. 117.

14. Stevens, *The Collected Poems*, op. cit. 464.

7. Sylvia Plath: The Illusion of a Greek Necessity
Ledbury Poetry Festival, 13 July 2013

1. William Scammell, ed., *Winter Pollen: Occasional Prose of Ted Hughes* (London: Faber & Faber, 1994), 178.

2. *Ariel: The Restored Edition*, A facsimile of Plath's manuscript, reinstating her original selection and arrangement, with a foreword by Frieda Hughes (London: Faber & Faber, 2004).

3. Sylvia Plath, *Collected Poems* (London: Faber & Faber, 1981), abbreviated as *CP* in my text. In the course of my talk at Ledbury I read aloud several of Sylvia Plath's poems that, for reasons of copyright, I am unable to print as part of this text.

4. Anne Stevenson, *Bitter Fame: A Life of Sylvia Plath* (New York: Houghton Mifflin; London: Viking Penguin, 1989), 298.